THE FIRST TO GO

The First to Go

by

Nabil Shaban

SIRIUS BOOK WORKS publishing

First published in Great Britain in 2007 by
Sirius Book Works publishing, 6 Vaucluse Place, Jackson
Street, Penicuik, EH26 9BF, Scotland, United Kingdom

ISBN 978-0-9548294-1-4 (from January 2007)
ISBN 0-9548294-1-7

A catalogue record for this book is available from the British
Library

Printed and bound in Scotland by Scotprint, Haddington

Front cover: "The First to Go", painting by Nabil Shaban
Title page: "Mercy Killing" by Nabil Shaban

Nabil Shaban was born in 1953 in Amman, Jordan and arrived in England when he was three for treatment for his osteogenesis imperfecta (brittle-bone disease). In 1980, he and Richard Tomlinson founded **Graeae** (pronounced Grey Eye), a professional theatre company of disabled performers. A writer and performer with many film and television credits, he is probably best known to television viewers for his role as ruthless intergalactic businessman Sil in the *Doctor Who* stories '**Vengeance on Varos**' and '**Trial of a Timelord**' (1985 + 1986).

On stage he has played Volpone, Hamlet, and Jesus in **Godspell**, Haille Sellassie in '**The Emperor** and Ayatollah Khomeini in **Iranian Nights**, played the storyteller Rashid in Salman Rushdie's "**Haroun and the Sea of Stories**", .Mack the Knife in Theatre Workshop's production of Brecht's "**Threepenny Opera**", ...for which he was nominated Critics' **Best Actor in Scottish Theatre** (2004-2005)

He has performed in such movies as **City of Joy** (1991), **Wittgenstein** (1992) and **Born of Fire** (1988), and on television in **Walter** (1982))and **Deptford Graffiti** (1991).

Since 1996, Nabil Shaban, a regular Theatre Workshop (Edinburgh) player, as a political actor, has worked in plays about Palestine (**The Little Lamp**, 1999 and **Jasmine Road**, 2003), about the State murder of Northern Ireland lawyer, Rosemary Nelson (**Portadown Blues**, 2000). Also "**D.A.R.E.**" (disabled terrorists opposed to genetic cleansing of disabled people) (1997-2004), **One Hour Before Sun Rise** (Ghazi Hussein 2006) about the systematic torture of Palestinian poet.

Shaban has written and presented several documentaries on themes of disability, including **Skin Horse** (1983), about disability and sexuality, the **Fifth Gospel** (1990), exploring the relationship between the Christian gospels and disability, **The Strangest Viking**" (2003), he argued the case that Ivarr the Boneless was a disabled viking leader.

In 1995, he founded *Sirius Pictures* to make video arts documentary **Another World**. This was followed in 1997 by the award-winning '**The Alien Who Lived in Sheds**' (1997) which he wrote, directed and starred in.. He also produced, wrote and directed the music film "**Crip Triptych**" for Scotland's 2006Triptych Music Festival.

Shaban's other plays include ""**I am the Walrus**" (about a schizophrenic who believes he made Mark Chapman assassinate John Lennon)

Nabil Shaban, who has a degree in Psychology and Philosophy, was awarded an honorary doctorate from the University of Surrey for the achievements of his career and his work to change public perceptions of disabled people.

In 2005 Nabil Shaban published his first book, "**Dreams My Father Sold Me**", an anthology of thirty years of his artwork and poetry, with a foreword by Lord Richard Attenborough.

Website: **http://uk.geocities.com/jinghiz53**   email: **Jinghiz53@yahoo.com**

6

For Tina Leslie.... who inspired me to create the character of Brunhilde.... and would have played the role specially written for her had the British medical profession not refused to cure her... of the Silicone Disease

....and for Jack Klaff, who suggested the title "First to Go"

....and Ewan Marshall, who as artistic director of the Graeae Theatre Company, agreed to commission me to write a play about the Disabled Holocaust.

Thanks to Robert Rae and Anne Flemyng of Theatre Workshop (Edinburgh) for arranging a rehearsed reading of "The First to Go" at the 2005 Edinburgh Fringe Festival.

NOTE: Regarding the song "Lili Marleen" which Brunhilde sings in the play. It was first sung in a Berlin cafe by Lale Andersen in 1938.
The words were by a Hamburg poet, Hans Leip and the music by Norbert Schultz.
Lale Andersen made a gramophone recording and in summer 1941 was played on German soldiers' radio station Belgrade, where it instantly became the most popular soldiers' song.

"If you know there is Evil afoot and you do nothing to stop it, then don't complain if you share the blame...and punishment."

- George

CONTENTS:

Author's Introduction

We all know about the millions of Jews who died in the Nazi extermination camps. Countless books, plays and films have been produced to ensure that we never forget and so remain vigilant against any likely recurrence. Yet there has never been a film which seeks to tell the story of Hitler's Euthanasia program for disabled people. In fact, the first to go, the First Victims, in Hitler's systematic drive to purify the Aryan race were people with physical, sensory, mental and psychiatric disabilities. Gas chambers were originally created to speed up the culling of such unwanted "Useless Eaters", the term used by Hitler to describe disabled people.

I am a disabled person, yet I did not even realise there was a "Disabled Holocaust" until I was in my late twenties in the early 80s. it was not something ever taught in history lessons about the Second World War, never featured in any movie about why Britain went to war against the Germans. Of course, as a child being educated in post-war Britain, I knew about the terrible systematic automated , factory-like slaughter of Jews. Even if non-Jews were not interested in making sure we never forgot Hitler's genocide of Jews, Jewish people were lucky that much of the world's literary, publishing, arts and entertainment industries were dominated by Jews and that there was a post-war-created-Israel to represent and advance Jewish interests, to ensure that Jews never experience such a threat of extinction again.

Sadly, disabled people have no such advantages. Disabled people are excluded from the mainstream of every field of human activity...except perhaps basket-making. We, disabled, are not in positions of power. We are not film or theatre directors or producers. We are not publishers and we don't own media conglomerates....so plays, books, films, television dramas don't get produced about the Disabled Holocaust. So most members of the public remain ignorant of how we were persecuted by Hitler who planned to wipe us from the face of the earth.

As a disabled actor and writer, on realising this, made a vow in 1983 to produce a film or play that would tell the story of the Disabled Holocaust...and, more importantly, from a disabled person's perspective.

At the time, I had so little self-confidence as a writer, I gave the idea of this unknown subject matter for a theatre play to a non-disabled actor/writer, Jack Klaff. He was a friend who had been extremely successful and famous for his one-person virtuoso shows on South Africa's apartheid system, psychoanalysis and Kafka. In the late 1980s and early 90s, with my permission, Jack went away to research material to write the play with me in the leading role. We thought we would approach Graeae, a professional theatre company of disabled performers (which I originally co-founded in 1980) to produce. I guess because Jack was very busy with his own projects (and probably not being disabled himself, he felt no sense of urgency), the play seemed to take forever to be written. I was complaining about this to someone in 1994, who said "Why don't you write it yourself. Its really your baby. You're disabled. Its your survival you are having to fight for. What better person to write this anti-Body Fascist play." I agreed and persuaded the new artistic director of Graeae, Ewan Marshall to apply for Arts Council funding to commission me to write the long-awaited play. Thankfully, the Arts Council of England agreed and in 1995 I got the commission to write "The First to Go" and in 1996 I completed the first draft, which is what you have in your hand.

It seems my life is often plagued by bad timing. No sooner had I written the first draft, than Ewan left Graeae for a better job elsewhere. The new Graeae director wasn't interested and so the play gathered dust as it received rejection after rejection from other theatre companies. The one bright light on the horizon was a commission from the British Film Institute to write a movie screenplay version, which I called "The Inheritance"...but no sooner did I complete the first draft of the film script, the Government abolished BFI production in 1997 and created the UK Film Council which seems only interested in supporting films that are mass appeal and simplistic enough to sell in America...so my film project bit the dust and languishes in a dark damp dank cellar.

Then, just when I had lost all hope of ever seeing "The First to Go" being produced, the Battersea Arts Centre, under the direction of Tom Morris, took interest and in 2002 we applied to a new disabled arts European Year of Disabled People funding scheme by the Government for a £50,000 grant. To my astonishment, we were awarded the dosh. But again, another case of bad timing, the bloody Blair government went and ruined everything by invading Iraq on March 19 2003. I had signed a contract with the Government, agreeing that neither party would do anything to bring the other party into ill repute. The British Government by illegally (and lying about Saddam's so-called "Weapons of Mass Destruction) invading and occupying Iraq was bringing me and my company into ill-repute. Because I totally opposed the war, I did not want to have my hands tied by a contract with the Government prohibiting me from any response, action or protest that the Government might construe as bringing it into ill repute, Because I was so disgusted with Blair's warmongering, I did not want the Government's "blood money", I handed back the £50,000 to 10 Downing Street. Needless to say, the British media, the Government backed BBC, CNN and other toadying USA media completely ignored my gesture, which shouldn't surprise anyone who knows that neither Britain nor America are genuine democracies.

It continues to be an uphill struggle to get this script whether as a stage play or feature film to a point of being produced.

I sent the script to the BBC Films but they wrote back, saying the subject matter of the Disabled Holocaust was not something that would have a wide enough appeal to the general audience. What makes me sick about this obvious "Body Fascist" attitude of the BBC, is that a two years after rejecting my script, they made yet another movie about the Jewish Holocaust, "Conspiracy" starring Kenneth Branagh. Why is it that the genocide of Jews is always considered of importance to the general public and the slaughter of disabled people is not? No one dares suggest that the Jewish Holocaust is a "bit old hat" and no longer relevant to present day.

I suspect one of the real reasons why institutions like the BBC and the Film Council refuse to make movies about the massacre of disabled people in Nazi Germany... is because Britain today still harbours ambitions of wiping out disabled people. This is evident by the following facts.

Genetic engineering science is encouraged in the pursuit of creating "the Perfect Baby". .Prospective Parents are continually pressurized by doctors, social services to have all pregnancies screened, so that disabled foetuses can be eliminated. The Fertilization and Embryology Bill 1988 allows disabled foetuses to be aborted, even if it reached full time. If the foetus isn't disabled then it would be a criminal offence to abort after 28 (or has it been reduced to 20 weeks?)...but when it comes to disability then its not a crime to kill a 9 month foetus. Clearly, there is one law for the disabled and another for the non-disabled. Very Nazi. There is no doubt in my mind, Britain through Thatcher and Blair, has become a Nazi country.

Blair's government is now trying to pass a law to allow the murder of old people in hospitals. We have also seen the prioritization system adopted by the National Health, whereby disabled people are refused life-saving surgical procedures. Children with Down's Syndrome not even allowed to go on waiting lists for vital heart surgery (Birmingham), severely disabled children refused life support and parents being prosecuted for obstructing hospital's attempts to kill (Portsmouth).

The BBC which is a Government funded (and therefore ultimately controlled) institution doesn't want to bite the hand that feeds it, so it will be reluctant to produce dramas that go against Government Nazi agendas. This, of course, doesn't just apply to disability. Everyone knows that the Blair government's invasion and occupation of Iraq is illegal, immoral and unjust, based on lies and hypocrisy...yet the BBC is too cowardly to force this point home and make Richard Attenborough or Ken Loach type dramas that are so desperately needed, in the fight against the increasingly undemocratic regime that is smothering the British people.

My play of Hitler's Euthanasia Program, "The First to Go" is a warning of the likely future for Britain's disabled people. I no longer trust any British government not to succumb and adopt Nazi eugenic ambitions. With the illegal wars in Iraq, Afghanistan and many more in the pipeline, our Rulers have developed an unsavoury taste for blood. - *Nabil Shaban 28/08/06*

THE FIRST TO GO   by Nabil Shaban

NOTE: All disabled characters must be played by disabled actors, and all the non-disabled characters played by non-disabled actors.
Also, No German accents!

Cast of Characters:

Disabled

GEORGE / Siegfried

JONAH / Dr. Gottfried Ewald / Claus von Stauffenberg

LUKE the Hypnotist / Josef Goebbels

BRIDGET / Heide

MICHAEL / Helmut

BRUNHILDE

Non-disabled

FRITZ / (Dr. Todt / Dr. Ernst Rudin / Dr. Gerhard Wagner / Prof. Ferdinand Saurbruch / Maj. Remer)

EVA / Dr. Dreck / Nina Stauffenberg / Magda Goebbels

KARL / (Dr. Spottgeburt / Prof. Alfred Hoche / Hitler/ Gen. Henning von Tresckow / Dr. Karl Brandt -T4)

ACT 1

Scene 1

(The Present Day. A Conference Hotel Room in Berlin, Germany)

The play starts in Darkness. A voice. Is it a Speaker at a Nazi Rally? Is it the Voice of Hitler?

SPEAKER: Now is the time. Now is your time! Now we must clear the ground for the Coming Race, the Herren Volk, the Race of Super Men....

MICHAEL: Is he hypnotized yet?

JONAH: Regressed.

MICHAEL: Is he regressed yet?

LUKE: Shhhhh.

SPEAKER: ....We must first rid Germany of inferior, physically and mentally degenerate Aryans. If we want beautiful and healthy flowers to grow in our garden then we must destroy all weeds which take all the goodness but give nothing in return. The Unproductive Consumers. The Useless Eaters! No, do not squeal at the harshness of my words. I am not the first to speak out. Did not that great British scientist, Sir Francis Galton, the father of eugenics, argue that with the selection of the finest and fittest specimens of humanity, we could eradicate physical and mental defects. Did not Charles Darwin in his brilliant book, "THE DESCENT OF MAN", cry out for the eugenic organisation of society. He spoke the God given truth when he said the care of the weak and sick members of society will lead inevitably to a serious degeneration of the human race. Nietzche, our Germany's very own genius who spoke for Zarathustra, proposed that only people with proper decent family histories be permitted to marry and that there be a **forbidding** of life to decadents, degenerates, that they must at all costs be **eliminated**. This GOD among thinkers wrote, and I quote "....society is not entitled to exist for its own sake, but only as a substructure and **scaffolding**, by means of which a select race of beings may elevate themselves to their higher duties, and, in general, a higher existence."

As the speech builds, a small spotlight appears on the SPEAKER's face - it gradually grows until it reveals the SPEAKER is disabled and in a wheelchair. It is GEORGE. The spot continues to grow to reveal he is in a room with 4 other disabled people, MICHAEL has **Down's Syndrome***, BRIDGET, has* **Cerebral Palsy***, LUKE ,has an* **impaired leg***, JONAH, has an* **amputated arm***, all watching and listening to him. They are fascinated because he has been hypnotically regressed to a past life he believes he once had.*

SPEAKER: (pause) No, I am not the First with this Vision.... But I AM THE FIRST with   the Will and the Power to see it through!

MICHAEL: Does he think he's Hitler?

LUKE;   Are you Adolf Hitler?

GEORGE: As German Aryans it is our duty, nay, our manifest destiny to create the Super Race. But this cannot be achieved whilst there is still one Cripple, Gypsy, Queer or Jew left on

21

	this planet. It is my privilege as your Fuhrer.....
BRIDGET:	I think its Hitler.
MICHAEL:	Oh shit!
GEORGE:	.....to inaugurate the first Biocracy in world history....
BRIDGET:	**Biocracy!**
MICHAEL:	What's that?
LUKE:	I suppose its a sort of biological and medical state with the doctors as high priests - in which the divine prerogative was that of cure through purification and revitalisation of the Aryan race....
MICHAEL:	Can't you talk English, Luke!
BRIDGET:	Shhhhhh!
GEORGE:	Our People's or Volkish State must see to it that only the healthy beget children. Here the state must act as the guardian of a millennial future. It must put the most modern medical means in the service of this knowledge. It must give racial leadership to our doctors, who - as cultivator of genes - biological soldiers - must declare unfit for propagation all who are in any way visibly sick or who have inherited a disease and can therefore pass it on....
BRIDGET:	The bloody tosser is referring back to the sterilization program, not the Euthanasia project.
JONAH:	Must be one of his early speeches.

LUKE: Fuhrer, are you only concerned with just the
               sterilizing of the socially inadequate? Surely
               that is not going to be enough?

GEORGE: All in good time. When we are at war then
               we can speak more openly of the planned
               elimination of the incurably ill. Believe me,
               the demands of war will smoothly facilitate
               the implementation of Genetic and Racial
               Hygiene. With the constant slaughter at the
               Front, the loss of favourite and healthy sons,
               will come the generally diminished sense of
               the value of human life. Then the Nation as
               one will realise that not only must it defend
               itself against the foreign enemy but also
               against degeneration. The people will lose
               their sentimentalism and will demand that we
               also make war on the feeble-minded, the
               epileptics, the mentally diseased, the blind,
               the deaf, the deformed, the cripples and the
               criminals. Our Nation in its darkest hour will
               value the shining truth that these pathetic
               creatures are inimical to the human race
               because they perpetuate their deficiencies
               and thus threaten the quality of the ensuing
               generations. Only in war will the Nation after
               having lost so much of its best blood ignore
               the Churches and its sloppy and effeminate
               Christian morality, and give us our Holy
               Mandate to exterminate these wretched
               undesirables.....

JONAH: Do we have to listen to any more of this
               filth? (to LUKE) Snap him out of it, will
               you.

LUKE: I can't just snap him out of it just like that. It
               has to be done gradually. If its not done
               properly I could do irreparable damage to his
               psyche.

JONAH:	Huh, I don't think anything you do will make him any more screwed up than he already was. Completely nuts .Fancy believing he was born disabled because of terrible crimes committed in a past life!
BRIDGET:	Listen, its not unusual to feel guilty about being disabled. Most of us at some time in our lives thinks its some kind of punishment sent by God or Karmic forces. If its not because of sins in this life or previous lives, then its because of sins of our fathers or mothers. From every angle, whether from religion, fairy tales, politics, fashion or medicine, we, the Disabled, are the Accused....
JONAH:	Well, I think it's all a load of Hoddle, if you ask me. I thought this hypnotism malarky was going to be a bit of a giggle. I mean, why couldn't George have been Cleopatra or Mata Hari or even Errol Flynn, then at least we could have had some entertaining smut.
BRIDGET:	Jonah, you're a prick! I don't know why you bothered coming to this Berlin Conference. You're not really serious about our War on Eugenics and Genetic Engineering!
LUKE:	Will you two please shut up! Have you no thought for George? I can't seem to get him back.
GEORGE:	....in a world composed of mongrels, defective and negroids all ideals of human beauty and nobility and all hopes of an idealized future for our humanity would be lost for ever.
LUKE:	On the count of 3, George, you are to forget Nazi Germany, leave Hitler and return to the

	body and mind of George Hamson, Berlin, 20th April... One...
JONAH:	(*whispers*) He told me last month he thought he had been Dr. Mengele! Now he' s Hitler! This bloody rubbish...
LUKE:	Two... You are beginning to wake now, George....
GEORGE:	On this planet of ours human culture and civilisation are indissolubly bound up with the presence of the Aryan. If he should be exterminated or subjugated then the dark shroud of a new barbarian era would enfold the earth.
LUKE:	THREE! Wake up George!
JONAH:	This is straight out of Hitler's MEIN KAMPF. This doesn't prove a thing.
LUKE:	Shut up. THREE, George. WAKE UP, GEORGE!
GEORGE:	...We must reinstate the free play of the forces which will......

(As GEORGE speaks, another voice in the darkness to the group's stage left, says the same lines. A spotlight reveals a non-disabled man, FRITZ, who steps forward into the light. None of the disabled group see him.)

FRITZ:	We must reinstate the free play of the forces which will lead the race through stages of sustained reciprocal education towards a higher type until finally the best portion of mankind will possess the world and even reach spheres...
GEORGE:	.....and reach planets, stars...

LUKE: GEORGE! Wake up. I will count to three
                 again.

FRITZ: ....reach stars that lie outside the earth.

GEORGE: We all feel that in the distant future, Man....

*(Another non-disabled speaker takes over GEORGE's
lines, a woman, EVA. She steps into the light on the
group's stage right)*

EVA: We all feel that in the distant future, Man
                 may be faced with problems which can be
                 solved only by a superior race of human
                 beings, a race destined to become masters of
                 all the other peoples and which have its
                 disposal the means and resources of the
                 whole world.

JONAH: Regurgitated MEIN KAMPF, that's all this
                 is. Bloody parlour games.

BRIDGET: Jonah, you make me sick. George is in
                 serious trouble. I'm going to get help. Find
                 someone who knows what they're doing.

LUKE: Its alright Bridget, I can handle this. There's
                 no need to interfere. George! Again, on the
                 count of three....

BRIDGET: You can't handle it, Luke. You've bitten off
                 more than you can chew.

JONAH: Funny how these Reincarnationists when
                 supposedly hypnotically regressed are always
                 the big people. The Napoleons, the
                 Alexander the Greats, the Mary Queen of
                 Scots - never the little people, the
                 insignificant slave, the lowly peasant, the
                 char-woman. The victims. The poor bloody
                 nobodies who don't have big enough egos for
                 the egos of the Reincarnationists to inhabit.
                 What about the victims George? How about

	telling their unsung stories! Too bloody boring for you, aren't they!
LUKE:	Jonah, shut the fuck up!
MICHAEL:	Yes, Jonah shut the fuck up!
BRIDGET:	Come on, Jonah. There must be a doctor or someone in this convention centre who can get us out of this mess.

(BRIDGET drags JONAH off stage.)

GEORGE:	We must recognise that the capacity for creating cultural values is essentially based on race....

(A third non-disabled actor steps forward. A middle-aged man, KARL as SPOTTEGEBURT, in a white coat with a stethoscope about his neck. He continues GEORGE's speech)

KARL:	We must recognise that the capacity for creating cultural values is essentially based on race and that the paramount purpose of the state is to prescribe and improve the race; for this is an indispensable condition of all progress in human civilisation.
FRITZ:	Illness, a disgrace to be managed by health control. Misery can only be removed from the world by painless extermination of the miserable. This process belongs to the physician - thus - doctors will be the true saviours of mankind.
EVA:	Good morning, Dr. Spottgeburt. I am pleased to report that in the 3 years since the Fuhrer passed the first sterilising laws - we have sterilized nearly a quarter of a million social undesirables. Compare that with a mere 20,000 in thirty years of sterilizing in the United States. I think we can safely, and if I

may be so bold, proudly say that we Germans have finally overtaken the English and the Americans in the Eugenics Movement.

SPOTTGEBURT: Excellent news, Dr. Eva Dreck! May I call you Eva?

EVA: If I can call you Adolf!

SPOTTGEBURT: *(Laughs)* Ha ha ha. Very good. Such blasphemy. How delicious it is, too.

(KARL/Spottgeburt and EVA kiss and rub against each other)

GEORGE: National Socialism is nothing but applied biology.

LUKE: Is this Hitler speaking?

GEORGE: No, Rudolf Hess.

LUKE: George, are you messing me about?

GEORGE: The Fuhrer holds the cleansing of the medical profession far more important than, for example, that of the bureaucracy since in his opinion the duty of the physician is or should be one of racial leadership.

LUKE: Hess again?

GEORGE: No, Martin Bormann.

LUKE: George, what is going on? Are we dealing with multiple personalities here?

MICHAEL: He's a channel!

LUKE: What?

MICHAEL: A channel. Like a television. He's moving across all the channels. He's filling up with ghosts. Berlin ghosts. He's attracting them.

LUKE:	Don't be silly, Michael. He's just fooling around. Eh George. You've been playing games with us.
GEORGE:	(*starts to sing "Lili Marlene"*) "Underneath the lantern, By the barrack gate...."
LUKE:	Come on, George. A joke's a joke.
GEORGE:	"Darling I remember the way you use to wait....."
LUKE:	George, I've had enough. I'm leaving you to it.

(LUKE leaves the stage. GEORGE oblivious, still trance-like, sings the first lines again)

GEORGE:	"Underneath the lantern, By the barrack gate...."

(MICHAEL goes up to GEORGE and puts his arms around him and holds him, rocking him gently)

MICHAEL:	It's alright George, Michael is still here. Michael won't leave you. St. George and St. Michael. Remember what you told me. We kill dragons.
GEORGE:	"Darling I remember the way you use to wait....."

(Another voice, female, takes up the song. A spotlight reveals the singer to be BRUNHILDE, a woman without hands and a severely scarred face)

BRUNHILDE:	(*sings*) "That was the time of early spring, When birds all sing and love was king, Of my heart and Marlene, Of my heart and Marlene."

(BRUNHILDE continues to softly hum the tune during the next section of dialogue)

EVA: Dr. Ernst Rudin, here are the latest figures. As you can see we have identified nearly half-a-million patients in institutions for sterilization ; 200,000 mental handicaps, 80,000 schizophrenics....

BRUNHILDE: "Time would come for roll call, Time for us to part....."

EVA: 20,000 manic depressives, 60,000 epileptics, 600 Huntingdon's Chorea.....

FRITZ: Is that all? Just 600? Must be more.

EVA: Not all the questionnaires have come in yet, Herr Doktor. Some of the institution directors are holding back. They think there are more sinister motives behind the forms.

FRITZ: Resisting? Or just being slow? No matter. Either way, we will have to send the "Experts" round to help these recalcitrants with their form filling. Carry on Frau Doktor.

EVA: 4000 Hereditary Blindness, 16,000 Hereditary Deafness, 10,000 Hereditary Alcoholism, 20,000 Bodily malformations.....

FRITZ: We are including such crippled states as club foot, harelip and cleft palate?

EVA: Yes. All congenital physical deviations from the norm. Curvature of the spine...

FRITZ: However slight?

EVA: Yes Herr Doktor.

FRITZ: Good, good. In the case of women deemed to be "mentally defective" we will be removing the entire uterus.

SPOTTGEBURT: I understand the experiments with X-ray sterilisation are showing a lot of promise.

FRITZ: Yes. Soon we will have the most efficient and effective instruments for racial hygiene at our disposal. Let us praise and congratulate Hitler and the National Socialist rule for its decisive path-breaking step toward inhibiting the further penetration of the German gene pool by the congenitally ill and inferior.

BRUNHILDE: "Darling I caress you and press you to my heart,
And in the power of lantern's light,
I hold you tight as on our last night,
My Lili of the Lamp-light,
My own Lili Marlene."

(The light changes colour from yellow to blue on GEORGE and MICHAEL as they continue to rock. The spot shrinks to just encircle them. BRUNHILDE also has her own spot, as she tells us her story)

Scene 2

BRUNHILDE: La la la la.... Until I was 6 years old, we lived in the remoter outskirts of Baden Baden where there were just scattered, isolated farmhouses. There I would be fascinated by the dark woods of the Black Forest that began near our house. From early on I was always a bit of a tomboy and a loner. I was always trying to escape and be swallowed up by the dark greenness, even though I was really forbidden to go into the forest alone. Many a time I would hide at bed time among the tall pines and listen to my parents call out "Brunhilde, Brunhilde. Come, quick or the gypsies will get you!" Actually when I was younger, some travelling gypsies did find me playing by myself but they didn't kidnap me. They just found a neighbour who brought me back home. I was disappointed really. I'd have loved to have been a gypsy dancing girl with all those horses, caravans, camp fires. A bit romantic, I know. But tell me a small boy who didn't want to run away to the circus, or little girl who didn't want to be a gypsy fortune teller.

(FRITZ, now a nursing orderly, enters. He approaches GEORGE and MICHAEL, separates the pair and starts to undress MICHAEL who becomes HELMUT as institution pyjamas are put on - Meanwhile BRUNHILDE pauses in her story to watch the following scene)

Scene 3

Early Morning. *FRITZ drags HELMUT out of bed and shakes him roughly.*

FRITZ: You've wet your bed again!

HELMUT: No.

FRITZ: YES! What's this? Smell it. Go on, smell it. Feel it. Its wet and its YOUR stink!

HELMUT: I didn't mean to. I'm sorry.

FRITZ: You said that yesterday. And the day before. You haven't stopped wetting the bed, filthy pig, since you've been here!

HELMUT: I'm sorry. I won't do it again. I promise.

FRITZ: Being sorry isn't good enough. Your promises are SHIT! How many times must we beat you? Do you like being beaten?

HELMUT:	No.
FRITZ:	No. Well, we won't beat you today.
HELMUT:	Good.
FRITZ:	It doesn't seem to stop you wetting the bed does it?
HELMUT:	No.
FRITZ:	No. So what are we going to do?
HELMUT:	Don't know.
FRITZ:	Buzz Buzz Sizzle Sizzle. Say it.
HELMUT:	Buzz Buzz Sizzle Sizzle.
FRITZ:	That's right. Buzz Buzz Sizzle Sizzle. Electric shock punishment for you, my boy.
HELMUT:	NO! P L E A S E. NOOOOO!

(HELMUT screams as FRITZ drags him off stage to the Electric Shock Room)

BRUNHILDE: When I wasn't playing in the forest I was in the company of horses in farmers' byres and stables. I never tired of stroking or grooming and talking to them. The farmers would be anxious as I crept between the horses' legs while I brushed them, never to this day has an animal kicked or bitten me.

(FRITZ returns with a pile of inmates' pyjamas and starts to undress the 1990's clothes from GEORGE, who sullenly becomes SIEGFRIED. Again BRUNHILDE pauses to watch.)

BRUNHILDE: I suppose I developed into a solitary child, and was never happier than when playing or working alone and unobserved. I could never bear being watched by anybody.

33

(BRUNHILDE pauses to watch FRITZ, who is struggling with the removal of SIEGFRIED's trousers, who is deliberately making it difficult. FRITZ turns and looks at BRUNHILDE)

FRITZ: Brunhilde, if you're not doing anything, can you assist me with Siegfried here. The little sod is deliberately being awkward.

BRUNHILDE: Let me just finish washing the laundry - *(to the audience)* Water. I've always loved water. It has this weird irresistible attraction for me. Even today, I seem to be perpetually washing and bathing. Especially after my accident. I seem to have become even more obsessed about keeping clean. I have to have my war on germs. Its the only thing that keeps me sane nowadays.

(FRITZ has finally managed to get SIEGFRIED into his pyjamas. EVA enters.)

EVA: Fritz, get the patients ready. *(Exits)*

FRITZ: Yes, Herr Doctor! *(mutter)* Shit!

BRUNHILDE: My mother and father were devout Catholics and loved me very much. There was a deeply religious atmosphere that pervaded our family life. I took my religious duties very seriously. I prayed with true, child-like gravity and asked God to let me be a sister of mercy in gloomy but exciting jungles of darkest Africa, or a nurse in the brave German army - *(sings)* "Underneath the Lantern, By the Barrack gate..."

(FRITZ has started to undress SIEGFRIED again, who is still being obstructive. FRITZ would dearly love to hit him, but SIEGFRIED is no HELMUT)

BRUNHILDE: God granted me my second wish. I became
               an Army nurse..... But perhaps you shouldn't
               ask God for things. Because sometimes his
               gifts can have a sting in the tale. (*pause*) God
               forbid that I say such things!

*(FRITZ having finally succeeded in stripping
SIEGFRIED **naked**, exits, leaving him shivering in the
middle of the stage.)*

BRUNHILDE: I will never forget my first love. Of course he
               was a soldier I nursed. He was shot through
               the knee and I fell hopelessly in love with
               him. I won't tell you his name. I bestowed
               such loving attention on him. I would caress
               him tenderly which at first made him feel a
               little nervous, and I would hold him up and
               support him, perhaps longer than was strictly
               necessary. Bit by bit, he responded to my
               love and one night behind some screens....I...
               we... (*pause*) ..we.. (*softly sings*) "Darling I
               caress you and press you to my heart"

*(FRITZ re-enters with HELMUT, who is also completely
naked. Having positioned HELMUT alongside
SIEGFRIED, FRITZ exits)*

BRUNHILDE: Our love was to be short-lived. Two weeks
               later he was discharged fit for continuing
               active service and was killed when his truck
               rode over a land mine....

*(FRITZ re-enters, escorting a third disabled patient
(cerebral palsy), female, HEIDE (previously BRIDGET).
HEIDE is also completely naked. All three patients are
lined up, waiting for DOCTOR SPOTTGEBURT and his
MEDICAL STUDENTS to do the rounds.)*

HELMUT: Why don't we have ice-cream anymore?

FRITZ: Be quiet. Children must be seen, not heard.

HELMUT: And why am I always hungry? I never use to
               be hungry.

FRITZ: Shut it, I said! The Doctors are coming.
               (*turns to look at BRUNHILDE*)

HELMUT: I'm not a child.

BRUNHILDE: I was given little time to grieve. Three days
               later our hospital hit by a bomb. I'd ignored
               the air raid warning to run for the shelter.
               One of the patients was refusing to go. He
               suffered terribly from claustrophobia. I
               volunteered to stay behind with him. I was
               convinced we would be lucky and be missed
               by the bombs. I've always been lucky in the
               past - that is, until... he... well... I suppose it
               was time for my luck to run out... as you can
               see. I should have died. I sometimes wish I
               had. But I didn't. And here I am. And here I
               must make the best of it. No good crying
               over spilt milk.

FRITZ: BRUNHILDE!

BRUNHILDE: Coming!

*(BRUNHILDE and FRITZ stand behind the line of
HELMUT, SIEGFRIED and HEIDE, waiting for the
DOCTORS to appear)*

(SILENCE as they wait)

HELMUT: And why am I always hungry? I never use to
               be hungry.

*(BRUNHILDE puts a comforting arm on HELMUT's
shoulder. FRITZ notices and shakes his head
disapprovingly)*

FRITZ: Shut it, I said! The Doctors are coming.

*(DR. SPOTTGEBURT (Karl) and DR. EVA DRECK
enter, accompanied by psychiatrist, DOCTOR.
GOTTFRIED EWALD (Jonah), who has only one arm -
lost during World War One)*

EWALD: But what about the Hippocratic Oath we all
                swore. Christian medical ethics? What has
                happened to "treatment unto death"?

SPOTTGEBURT: My dear Doktor Ewald, the ill-conceived
                "love of thy neighbour" has to disappear. I'm
                afraid such outmoded concepts as charity and
                compassion are anathema to National
                Socialist medical doctrine. Under the New
                Order it is the supreme duty of the state to
                grant life and livelihood only to the healthy
                and hereditarily sound.

EWALD: I don't think I can get use to this new way of
                thinking.

SPOTTGEBURT: My dear Gottfried, you have to, you must.
                I can understand it must be more difficult for
                you. Your own unique situation will
                doubtless colour your feelings. It was during
                the Great War you lost your arm? Yes?

EWALD: Yes.

SPOTTGEBURT: Quite. But even so, we, doctors, above all
                must become hardened - if he or she - (*nods
                to EVA*) is to adopt the ice-cold logic of the
                necessary. The individual has meaning only
                in the light of the ultimate aim of a racially
                pure people.

*(The Trio of Doctors walk up to examine the patients.
SPOTTGEBURT roughly manhandles HELMUT, moving
his head from side to side)*

SPOTTGEBURT: Besides, these people are not normal
                human beings. One cannot speak to them as I

can speak to you. They don't laugh. They are
all high grade imbeciles, mongols, spastics.
The medical term for this one?

(SPOTTGEBURT prods HEIDE and looks at EVA)

EVA: Cerebral polio, Herr Doktor.

SPOTTGEBURT: Prognosis?

EVA: Incurable.

SPOTTGEBURT: Precisely. And this one? *(points to
                Siegfried)*

EVA: Achondroplasia?

SPOTTGEBURT: Dwarfism? Not bad but not quite. No
                doubt you were mislead by the scoliosis, the
                severe curvature of the spine....

*(SPOTTGEBURT has FRITZ turn SIEGFRIED onto his
stomach, so that his back, arse and genitals are in full
view - a totally degrading position to be in. EWALD and
BRUNHILDE)*

SPOTTGEBURT: He has a very rare condition.
                Osteogenesis Imperfecta.

EVA: Ah, brittle bones!

SPOTTGEBURT: Good girl! Normally his kind die at birth.
                But this one slipped through the net, didn't
                he...

*(SPOTTGEBURT pats SIEGFRIED on the buttocks and
then points to his genitals)*

SPOTTGEBURT: Notice the genitalia is quite normal. In fact
                he is surprisingly rather well endowed.
                Which, believe it or not, is quite normal for
                male specimens of his kind. Dwarfs too, are
                disproportionately well endowed. Such a
                waste. Yet another cruel trick of nature. Such

a pity he will never have the opportunity to take full advantage. Even so, no woman in her right mind would let him pollute her genes. Wouldn't you agree Frau Doktor Dreck?

EVA: Heaven forbid! It would be a crime against humanity.

SPOTTGEBURT: Now there speaks a true German woman. *(affectionately pats EVA's bottom)*

SPOTTGEBURT: *(to FRITZ)* Has he been....?

FRITZ: Been? Oh yes, he did a very good motion this morning.

SPOTTGEBURT: Imbecile! I am not talking shit!

(SIEGFRIED mouths silently "Oh yes you are", much to the surprise and amusement of EWALD and BRUNHILDE)

FRITZ: Oh! That! No. I'm afraid the X-ray machine has broken down again. We've been having a lot of problems with controlling the level of dosages. Its either too much or too little....

SPOTTGEBURT: Well if you must err, err on the side of "too much".

EWALD: Excuse me, Dr. Spottgeburt, I have another meeting to attend. Must dash. Hope you don't mind?

SPOTTGEBURT: Nooo. Of course not, my dear chap. I hope our little tete a tete has clarified a few things, put your mind at rest, set you on the right path!

EWALD: Yes, yes. Its been extremely - um - illuminating.

(EWALD rushes off stage left. SPOTTGEBURT surveys the group one last time and...)

SPOTTGEBURT: Come. *(...marches off stage right with EVA and FRITZ)*

(SIEGFRIED gives SPOTTGEBURT "the finger" behind his retreating back)

Scene 4

(BRUNHILDE helps the patients to dress)

HELMUT: What's your name?

BRUNHILDE: Brunhilde. What's yours?

HELMUT: Helmut.

BRUNHILDE :   How can he get away with treating you like that. As if you were some dumb animal?

SIEGFRIED: That's exactly it. That is exactly how he sees us. Dumb animals. Its quite normal. That's how most doctors see us. Its inherent in medical training. The doctors are trained to be authoritarian, nationalistic.....

HEIDE: ...Elitist, supercilious....

HELMUT: ....Snobby, bossy...

SIEGFRIED: ...clinical, cold-blooded. I've had a life time of them and they're all bastards.

BRUNHILDE: But you're not dumb animals. You can talk. Why don't you say something to him. Let him hear you speak. Let him know you've got a mind, you've got feelings just like him.

HEIDE: What if you can't talk. You're still human.

SIEGFRIED: Anyway, what's the point. I could talk until I'm blue in the face. He won't hear me. He

40

doesn't want to. It would contradict his world view, his "Weltanschnung". If I was to spout Hegelian dialectics at him, he would pass it off as mere parroting - linguistic juggling without human comprehension!

HELMUT: You're new aren't you.

BRUNHILDE: Yes I came yesterday.

SIEGFRIED: Are you one of us - a patient, or one of them?

HEIDE: The Enemy...

BRUNHILDE: Well...I...um... I am on the staff but they treat me as if I'm one of you...

HEIDE: Like scum...

HELMUT: Poor little Cinders...

BRUNHILDE: Well, I didn't quite mean... Its not that bad.

HEIDE: Early days.

SIEGFRIED: That's okay. You've got the uniform. If you know what I mean. The Mark of Cain. So you count as one of us. When they come to sort the sheep from the goats, they'll throw you in with us. You're an unpleasant reminder of their own mortality. They want to be perfect, but they can't be. And anything or anyone that contradicts such yearnings is mercilessly crushed, annihilated, removed from their presence.

HELMUT: We don't wear badges. We don't need to. Our bodies are our badges.

BRUNHILDE: I don't know what you're talking about?

HEIDE: Don't worry. Neither do we really. We think we do. We tell each other stories, to try to make sense of what's happening to us....

HELMUT:	They are doing things to us.
HEIDE:	Over the last few years, we have had to undergo lots of strange operations. They took something from me last year. I have a cut on my stomach. An appendix they said. But I think I know what they took but I try not to think about it. I can't think about the emptiness that now grips my insides.
HELMUT:	Friends have gone.
HEIDE:	Disappeared. Been taken away. To a better sanatorium they say. In the country. Lots of fresh air, flowers, trees. I've been doing a lot of reading lately. Certain books. Books to help me understand. To know....
SIEGFRIED:	"To be fore-warned is to be fore-armed", so they say.
HELMUT:	How can you have four arms? I don't want to be a freak.
HEIDE:	So we make up stories. Its the best way to pool our resources. To help us understand.
SIEGFRIED:	Its also entertainment for us.
HEIDE:	We have this rather superstitious idea that perhaps if we tell the stories properly, with the right power, we can somehow affect our own destiny - the future. We can change events...
HELMUT:	Are we going to do a new story? Now that she's with us? What's your name again?
BRUNHILDE:	Brunhilde. I can remember your name. It's Helmut.
HELMUT:	What's his name?
BRUNHILDE:	I don't know. He hasn't told me.

HELMUT:	Siegfried.
BRUNHILDE:	The Dragon-slayer!

(FRITZ enters unnoticed)

HELMUT:	Fafnir!

(FRITZ slaps HELMUT)

FRITZ:	Hey, no swearing!
HELMUT:	I'm not swearing. Fafnir's not swearing.
SIEGFRIED:	Piss off Fritz.
BRUNHILDE:	Fafnir is the name of the dragon in the Volsung saga.
FRITZ:	I know! And who are you? Queen of the Valkeries? Mistress of the Scavengers? Collector of the Dead. You'd better watch her, Siegfried, Brunhilde will be the death of you, ha ha ha. Anyway it's time for bed.
HELMUT:	They love each other.
FRITZ:	*(looking sharply at BRUNHILDE)* Already. God, you're fast!
HELMUT:	Not them, stupid! Brunhilde and Siegfried in the story!
FRITZ:	Who are you calling stupid?

(FRITZ goes forward to slap HELMUT again but BRUNHILDE steps between them)

BRUNHILDE:	Please. No. Fritz. Why don't you let me put them to bed tonight? I've got to learn the ropes anyhow.
FRITZ:	Oh alright. Listen Brunhilde. I wouldn't get too attached to them if I were you. There's no future in it for you. Bad investment. *(to the patients)* Brunhilde is taking care of you

43

tonight. So behave yourselves. I want you all
in bed in five minutes.

(FRITZ exits)

SIEGFRIED: Mono-testicular toe-rag!

(BRUNHILDE prepares everyone for bed)

BRUNHILDE: Have we always been the Enemy?

SIEGFRIED: We?

BRUNHILDE: I was a nurse before the accident.

HELMUT: What happened to you? Did you fall over?

BRUNHILDE: I'll tell you about it another day.

SIEGFRIED: Probably not. I was never conscious of it -
                until....

HELMUT: ...the Bad Man came.

BRUNHILDE: The Bad Man? You mean Doktor
                Spottgeburt?

HELMUT: No. **THE** BAD MAN. The Bad Man behind
                all the Bad Men.

BRUNHILDE: You mean Satan? Lucifer?

HELMUT: Who?

HEIDE: No, the Bad Man who is in our story. The
                Evil Genius who operates the machinery.

SIEGFRIED: The Dark Alchemist who cannot transmute
                his bleak heart into gold so he collects and
                mixes the unholy ingredients of hate, death
                and despair, and infects others with his
                poisonous contagion...

HEIDE: The Master Hypnotist who turned those who
                should protect and heal us, or care for us, into
                the Enemy.

SIEGFRIED:	Nah. He just brought out what was already lying dormant in them. They say a hypnotist can never force you to do what you don't want to do.
BRUNHILDE:	Who are we actually talking about?
HELMUT:	I told you, silly! The Bad Man in our story.
HEIDE:	Do you want to join our Story Circle?
BRUNHILDE:	What do I have to do?
HEIDE:	Everyday for half an hour, sometimes even an hour....
HELMUT:	If it gets exciting...
HEIDE:	We take it in turns to tell part of a huge story....
SIEGFRIED:	An Epic of global proportions, of lies, cowardice, deceit, courage and sacrifice...
BRUNHILDE:	What about Love? Romance?

(Embarrassed silence)

HEIDE:	If you want. It depends on whose turn it is to tell the story. If its your turn you can introduce anything you like. The story can go anywhere. From one day to the next, we never know where it will lead.
HELMUT:	Can we do a new story? I don't like the Bad Man story.
SIEGFRIED:	No. We must see it through. *(to BRUNHILDE)* Anyway you'd better put us to bed otherwise you'll be in trouble.

Scene 5

(BRUNHILDE turns to the audience)

BRUNHILDE:	Well, I did join their Story Circle. At first I felt a bit uneasy. I was worried about who this Bad Man was. It all smelt a bit treasonable to me. But after a few days I relaxed into it and accepted it for what it was - a child's play. A fantasy. To while away the hours. Although I did wish they could have chosen a more cheerful story. Whenever it was my turn to continue the telling, I did try to move it on more positive directions but as soon as the others took over, especially Siegfried, the fable returned to its dark and gloomy course.
SIEGFRIED:	It wasn't long before all the doctors and nurses in the land did what the Bad Man wanted...
HELMUT:	Except for Doctor Ewald...
SIEGFRIED:	Yes, except for Doctor Ewald, and perhaps a few others. But most, gleefully followed his laws which were passed six months after he came to power...
HELMUT:	To cut off our willies and sew up our fannies...
BRUNHILDE:	HELMUT!
HELMUT:	Its true, isn't it Siegfried?
SIEGFRIED:	Yes, Helmut, in our story it is. *(points to HEIDE)*
HEIDE:	My turn! At the same time, hospitals were encouraged to neglect patients; each year funds were reduced and state inspections of standards were suspended. De-regulation was the in-word. Even so, the Bad Man would send his Bully Boys....
HELMUT:	Men in Black.

HEIDE:	To show government officials, students, newspaper men, police around to laugh and poke fun at us. Point at our funny walks, accuse us of repulsive behaviour, calls us names - "human ballasts" - "empty shells" - "zombies" - "the living dead"....
HELMUT:	But he did like animals, children and was a vegetarian. That was my bit.
BRUNHILDE:	Who?
HELMUT:	The Bad Man. I wanted him to like animals.
SIEGFRIED:	He only likes some children, remember.
HELMUT:	He doesn't like brown children?
SIEGFRIED:	Nope.
HELMUT:	Yellow children?
SIEGFRIED:	Nope.
HELMUT:	*(upset)* Black children, children who can't walk or see or hear? Children who talk differently, who think differently?
SIEGFRIED:	Nope. None of them.
HELMUT:	What children does he like?
SIEGFRIED:	You know. Only those who are as white as snow, with blond hair, blue eyes, who can run and jump and kiss his arse.
BRUNHILDE:	Siegfried, is this story really necessary?
HELMUT:	Shhhh. It's still Heidi's go.
HEIDE:	It wasn't long before all the wise men and all the professors agreed with the Bad Man's dreams and tried to persuade him to go further, even though he didn't need persuading. He had already made his Master

plan years before - but he encouraged them to think they had thought of it first. That way the guilt could be spread more evenly and possible resistance isolated.

(FRITZ steps into the light)

SIEGFRIED: Your name?

FRITZ: Professor Walter Schultz. Bavarian Health Commissioner. Ultimately, more radical measures are going to be needed. I have written to the Fuhrer about this. Sterilization is insufficient. Psychopaths, the mentally retarded and other inferior types must be isolated and killed. This policy has already been initiated in our concentration camps.

(KARL steps into the light)

KARL: Professor Alfred Hoche. Freiburg. Let me stress that some killing is compassionate and medically ethical, particularly where such people suffer various forms of psychiatric disturbance, brain damage or retardation. These killings are allowable useful acts, since we are talking about people who are already dead. I should also remind you that these people create a terrible economic burden especially if their gross mental and physical deficiencies are going to require a lifetime of institutionalization. The State must abandon and push out less valuable members.   We, physicians, are best qualified for making correct selections using proven scientific criteria to establish the impossibility of improvement of a mentally dead person. However, we physicians, if we are to carry out such duties, must be legally protected.

(FRITZ steps forward again)

HELMUT:	Name?
FRITZ:	I'm not talking to you. You don't exist.
HELMUT:	*(Shouts)* NAME? I'm telling the story!
FRITZ:	Gerhard Wagner. Godfather of the Euthanasia Program.

(FRITZ turns to KARL and EVA)

FRITZ:	I was talking with the Fuhrer the other day at Nurenburg and he assures me that he appreciated the tremendous burden on relatives, the general population and the medical profession by the mentally ill and other inadequates. He has instructed me to discuss with high ranking officials and doctors the plan to kill idiotic children and mentally ill people. Josef Goebbels, the Reich Propaganda Minister, is to commission more films which will demonstrate the misery of such poor unfortunates' lives.

(DR. EWALD steps forward)

SIEGFRIED:	Name and year?
EWALD:	Doktor Gottfried Ewald. 1938. An insidious campaign has been started by the SS, which is carefully encouraging, nurturing and orchestrating requests from relatives of new borns or very young infants with severe deformities and brain damage for granting mercy killings.
HEIDE:	The Bad Man was pleased. He personally received and approved these requests. The first letter he received which started the ball rolling was the petition for the "mercy killing" of an infant named....

EWALD:	....Knauer. Born blind, with one leg missing and part of one arm, and allegedly "idiot". The grandmother wrote the original request, although the father and mother were made the petitioners.
HEIDE:	The Bad Man was deeply moved by the dear, sweet, old grandma's plea. He immediately wrote to his trusty physician and confidant....
HITLER *(Karl)*:	My dear Karl. This Knauer child sounds positively horrendous. Something must be done to put it out of its misery. I want you to go to the university of Leipzig where it is hospitalized, to determine whether the information in the petition is accurate. Consult with the physicians there and if the facts given by the parents are correct, you are, in my name, to inform them that they can carry out euthanasia. You are empowered to tell these physicians that any legal proceedings against them will be quashed by my order.
EVA:	I couldn't believe it. Hitler's own personal doctor in our house. It was right here, Karl Brandt was standing near the window. He was tall, good-looking and impressive. He in his early thirties. He seemed to fill up the whole room. He explained to us that the Fuhrer had personally sent him, and that our son's case interested the Fuhrer very, very much. The Fuhrer wanted to explore the problem of people who had no future - whose life was worthless. From then on, we wouldn't have to suffer from this terrible misfortune because the Fuhrer had granted us the mercy putting to sleep of our son. Later, we could have other children, handsome and healthy, of whom the Reich could be proud.

Germany had to be built and every bit of energy would be required. That's what Herr Brandt explained to us. He was a proud man - intelligent, very convincing. He was like a saviour to us - the man who could deliver from us a very heavy burden. We thanked him and told him how grateful we were.

FRITZ: It is the Fuhrer's wish that the Euthanasia Project be understood as a responsible medical process and parents are not to feel personally responsible for the death of their children.

KARL: Now this is strictly confidential but for the purposes of clarification of scientific questions in the field of congenital malformation and mental retardation, I want registration of all children suspected of the following hereditary diseases - idiocy and mongolism, especially when associated with deafness, microcephaly, hydrocephaly, malformations of all kinds, especially of limbs, head and spinal column and paralysis, including spastic conditions.

FRITZ: Are we to register minor physical impairments?

KARL: Er.. Yes. Just to be on the safe side. Once we receive the reports I will head a three man team which will study them and decide which children should be put down. In the column headed "treatment" we will mark either a plus or positive sign - meaning death, or a minus or negative sign - meaning life, or if there is any uncertainty and further observation is required. But I don't think we will be troubled with too many of those.

EVA: We will provide a service as close to families
                as possible, thus saving in money and
                transportation costs. Also parents are likely
                to be more amenable to accepting necessary
                transfers. We will, of course, tell parents that
                their child will receive the best and most
                modern therapy available.

SIEGFRIED: Ah Mr. Rudin. And how are you Mrs. Rudin?

(EVA and FRITZ turn and approach SIEGFRIED)

SIEGFRIED: Now there is nothing for you to worry about,
                but it might be necessary to perform a
                surgical operation that could possibly have
                an unfavourable result.

*(HEIDE approaches EVA from behind and taps her on
the shoulder)*

HEIDE: Frau Heinz? The ordinary therapy may no
                longer help, so extraordinary therapeutic
                measures will have to be taken. Your child is
                exceedingly excitable. The most extreme
                case of idiocy we have seen in years, I have
                to say.

SIEGFRIED: We are unable to keep her quiet with the
                normal dose of sedatives, so we will have to
                use an overdose in order to avoid
                endangering the poor thing through her own
                restlessness. Unfortunately these extreme
                therapies can be fatal but the extraordinary
                problems of your child leave us no choice.

KARL: Parents reluctant to give consent will be told
                they should be grateful, given the seriousness
                and incurability of their child's disability,
                that they are to be given the best and
                efficacious treatment available. If parents
                continue to resist we will inform them that it
                is impossible to delay or cancel the transfer.

We may have to warn them that their guardianship will be withdrawn. Finally, if that fails then the threat of calling a parent up for special labour duty. But I suspect only rarely will we have to resort to this. The vast majority of people have complete confidence in the medical profession and are unlikely to question our practices.

Scene 6

(The Story Circle continues)

HEIDE: And so all across the land thousands of parents, midwives, district medical officers, nurses, doctors, psychiatrists, many perhaps unwittingly, help the Bad Man...

HELMUT: King Herod....

HEIDE: ....in his slaughter of the Innocents. From his headquarters in Berlin...

HELMUT: Berlin! That's where we are!

HEIDE: ....he and his band of demon doctors secretly established a network of over 30 killing centres within hospitals, sanatoriums, special homes throughout Germany. First, it was the new-borns, then it was children up to three, and when the Bad Man became more confident, and nobody seemed to be complaining, even older children were included. And why did he want to kill all these special children?

HELMUT: Because he didn't like the look of them.

BRUNHILDE: If Looks can kill, they certainly will.

HEIDE:	Yes. The Bad Man dreamed he was a great artist. He thought he knew everything about form, shape, symmetry. He was a Classicalist. He was a Platonist. He wanted to bring the Perfect Forms down from Heaven. He yearned for the return of Atlantis. He hated anything that offended his visual sense of style, beauty. He hated Abstract Art, Modernism, Atonalism. To him, these children were just ugly bits of sculpture, badly made, amateur and decadent works of art, to be broken up and reshaped into objects more aesthetically pleasing.
EVA:	Before a child was killed, he or she - but perhaps I should say "it"... Well, it was so severely impaired. If you could have seen it. My god, such high grade defectives, we were having to deal with! It would be kept .... No... I will say child. She would be kept in the institution for a few weeks, to give the impression that she was being given some form of therapy. That was normally arranged by the director of the institution, in my case that was Herr Doktor Spottgeburt. The order was usually conveyed by innuendo rather than a specific instruction. It was often left to me to carry out the actual.... "treatment". It was generally done by means of luminal tablets dissolved in liquid such as tea. I would give the sedative repeatedly - in the morning and at night - over two or three days, until the child lapsed into a continuous sleep. The luminal dose would be increased until the child went into a coma and died. For those children who had difficulty drinking I would inject the luminal. If the luminal did not kill the child quickly enough as was often the case with hyper-active children who had

developed a high tolerance of the drug through having been given so much of it - then I would administer a fatal morphine-scopolamine injection. I would then have to list the death as having been caused by a more or less ordinary disease such as pneumonia or tuberculosis. I don't think it was murder. We were just putting to sleep. Doing it this way made it easier to go along with the program. Tablets, injections, children sedated, sleeping. It just felt like normal doctor duties. Had we'd been given direct orders to go from bed to bed shooting these children, then it would not have worked.

FRITZ: That would have felt like murder. This way we were just putting the little babes to sleep.

KARL: It is important, vital, that the killing doctors are not made to feel personally responsible for another human being. We must help them to feel that they are no more than a small cog in a vast, officially sanctioned medical machine.

HELMUT: I'm not a child am I?

SIEGFRIED: No.

HELMUT: And the Bad Man is only killing children?

SIEGFRIED: Yes.

Scene 7

HITLER (KARL): A shrewd ruler will always enforce his exactions on the populace only by stages. Then he may expect that a people who have lost all strength of character - which is

always the case with those that voluntarily
submits - will not find in any of these acts of
oppression, if one be enforced apart from the
other, sufficient grounds for taking up arms.
The more numerous the extortions thus
passively accepted so much less   will
resistance appear

*(JOSEF GOEBBELS / Luke enters, limping quite severely
which he struggles to inhibit as he approaches HITLER /
Karl)*

HITLER (KARL): It is incredible to think I wrote something
like this 15 years ago. Have you read "MEIN
KAMPF"?

GOEBBELS: Yes Fuhrer. Back in 1925. Fantastic piece of
writing.

HITLER (KARL): Uncannily prophetic, wouldn't you say!
First the theory, which I call the Salami
Theory, followed by its application.

GOEBBELS: Your word made flesh, mein Fuhrer.

HITLER (KARL): Slice by slice. Very thin slices at first,
barely perceptible. But nonetheless, more and
more of the sausage disappears. And no one
notices until, of course, it is too late. You
know I am a convinced Vegetarian. With me,
it is a matter of irrefutable principle. Are you
Vegetarian?

GOEBBELS: I am now, Fuhrer.

HITLER (KARL): I am convinced it will be the new world
religion of the future. You know, Man, who
is nothing really, should not feel so superior
to animals. He has no reason to. Man
believes that he alone has intelligence, a soul
and the power of speech. Has not the animal
these things?

GOEBBELS: *(slightly bemused, confused even)* Er....

HITLER (KARL):   Just because with our dull senses, we cannot
                   recognise them, it does not prove that they
                   are not there. If Homo Sapiens was to
                   disappear off the face of the earth tomorrow,
                   he wouldn't be missed.

HELMUT: I don't like this story anymore.

SIEGFRIED: We know. You said.

BRUNHILDE: Neither do I. I think it is sick.

SIEGFRIED: Well, you can change it when its your turn.

HEIDE: Lets call it a day. Fritz will be along soon,
                   anyway, to wrap us up for the night.

HELMUT: I don't want Fritz to put me to bed. I want
                   you to put me to bed, Brunhilde. Will you
                   sing to me like you did last night?

BRUNHILDE: Of course I will.

HELMUT: It's my turn to tell the story tomorrow. Can I
                   tell about the Liar?

HEIDE: If you want.

BRUNHILDE: The Liar?

HELMUT: He's the Bad Man's side-kick. Follows him
                   around like a puppy dog. He walks funny.
                   Like this.

(HELMUT exaggerates GOEBBEL's limping walk)

HELMUT: And he's small and thin, and all the other bad
                   men, the Bully Boys in Black, call him the
                   "Evil Dwarf", and he's got a funny shaped
                   head. Why didn't the Bad Man kill Jokey if
                   he looked so funny?

SIEGFRIED: If he had been a child when the Bad Man
               became king, he would have been killed.

HEIDE: Besides, he was the Liar. He was very clever
               and brilliant with words. He knew how to
               make the people believe the Bad Man was
               their Saviour, their God. Without the Liar,
               the Bad Man would have found it harder to
               persuade the people that bad was good, and
               good was bad.

(FRITZ marches in)

FRITZ: Okay all you vegetables, time to be bedded.

BRUNHILDE: I'll see to Helmut if you don't mind.

FRITZ: Fine.

*(FRITZ grabs SIEGFRIED's wheelchair and pushes him
to stage left)*

FRITZ: Siegfried, you never seem to want to play
               chess with me anymore?

SIEGFRIED: You've changed.

FRITZ: The damn job's changed. Between you, me
               and the Kaiser's willy, I'm thinking of
               putting in to go to the Front. I know you
               think I'm a vicious bastard sometimes but
               there are things afoot which I don't want to
               be a part of. I'd rather be a soldier and kill
               those who can fight back.

SIEGFRIED: What are you talking about? Is there
               something in store?

FRITZ: Nuff said, old chap. I have said more than is
               healthy for me to say.

*(FRITZ finishes with SIEGFRIED, and takes HEIDE off
stage.)*

(BRUNHILDE is sitting beside HELMUT who is now tucked up in bed)

BRUNHILDE: "Underneath the lantern, by the Barrack gate,
Darling I remember the way you use to wait,
That was the time of early Spring,
When birds all sing and love was king
of my heart and Marlene....."

HELMUT: *(interrupts)* I had a puppy dog called Marley,

BRUNHILDE: I didn't think they allowed pets here.

HELMUT: No, at home, when I lived with my Mum and Dad. But they got too old to look after me. Or I got too big for them. They weren't allowed to look after me anymore. So I came here. I hope Marley is alright.

BRUNHILDE: I'm sure he is. Hey, I had a pony when I was seven. He was coal black with sparkling eyes and a long mane.

HELMUT: What was his name?

BRUNHILDE: Claus. Because I got him on Christmas Day...

HELMUT: What do you mean?

BRUNHILDE: Santa Claus. Clever eh! He was my best friend ever. Followed me wherever I went, just like a puppy dog. When my parents were away, I would even take him up to my bedroom.

HELMUT: Your bedroom! You can't take a pony to bed with you! He's too big.

BRUNHILDE: Oh I didn't have him in bed, but he would sleep in the room. The servants never use to tell on me. Anyway my love, you must sleep.

(BRUNHILDE kisses HELMUT on the forehead)

BRUNHILDE: Good night my darling.

(SIEGFRIED who had been watching, calls
BRUNHILDE)

SIEGFRIED: Hey Brunhilde!

BRUNHILDE: What?

SIEGFRIED: Don't I get a "Good night" kiss?

BRUNHILDE: Certainly not. You're too old.

SIEGFRIED: I'm not much older than Helmut.

BRUNHILDE: Yes but he's - *(stops herself)* Oh alright. But
              behave.

(She bends to kiss him on the cheek but he turns his head
and kisses her on the lips. She doesn't pull away
immediately but when she does, she gives him a gentle
slap across the face)

BRUNHILDE: Hey, that's not a goodnight kiss!

SIEGFRIED: What is it, then?

BRUNHILDE: A snog and I don't know you well enough for
              that.

SIEGFRIED: Does that mean I've got something to look
              forward to when you do know me well
              enough?

BRUNHILDE: Say "Good night Brunhilde".

SIEGFRIED: Good night Gorgeous.

BRUNHILDE: You naughty man.

Scene 8

(HELMUT runs on stage. Stops, looks at his legs, first the
left, then the right. Twists his right foot and practices
limping around the stage. SIEGFRIED, HEIDE and

BRUNHILDE enter, see HELMUT and sit in the Story Circle)

HELMUT: It's my turn to tell the story. My name is Jokey Gobbler and I'm the Liar. Actually I shouldn't tell I'm the Liar because you won't believe anything I say. But then you won't believe me if I say I am the Liar. So you will believe everything I say, so I'm alright. I can say whatever I like. I was born on the moon.

EVERYONE: Liar!

HELMUT: Alright I wasn't born on the moon. I was born - Where was I born?

HEIDE: Rhheydt, in the Lower Rhine, near Dusselldorf.

HELMUT: *(grins)* Yes, in a dufflebag. Ha ha ha. My mum was Queen of Austria...

EVERYONE: Liar!

HELMUT: *(giggles)* Alright. My mum was a milk-maid and her name was Kate. My dad's name was Fritz... *(pauses to see if he is called "Liar", he then continues mischievously)* and he was a Wig-maker...

EVERYONE: **LIAR!**

HELMUT: WICK! I mean Wick Worker! Wick wick! He gets on my wick. Wick. Witch. Wicked. Which witch is wicked?

SIEGFRIED: Get on with it.

HELMUT: I wasn't born with a clubbed foot. It happened when I was 3 years old. I caught a disease called Ozzy - Ozzy...

(JOSEF GOEBBELS steps forward)

GOEBBELS: Osteomyelitis. My mother was devastated. Doctors, physiotherapists, masseurs did everything they could to rid my right leg of the creeping paralysis but it was hopeless. In the end, the experts just shrugged their shoulders and told my parents that my right foot was lamed for life, would fail to grow properly and develop into a clubbed foot. And I will always have to wear these ugly orthopaedic appliances.

HELMUT: Clap him in irons!

(HELMUT leads SIEGFRIED and HEIDE in giving GOEBBELS a slow hand-clap. BRUNHILDE giggles at HELMUT's witticism)

GOEBBELS: My mother, Katharina, was convinced this was a curse on the family. As far as she was concerned, any physical defect was a punishment inflicted by God. She would drag me off to church and I would have to kneel with her, and we'd pray fervently that the Lord might give me strength and cast this evil away from me and the family. Fearing the neighbour's gossip, she would claim that my deformity was not the result of illness but an accident. She would say that she picked me up from the bench without noticing that my foot was caught between the slats. As a matter of fact, that's what I say to people today. Especially those of my enemies in the party who are forever seeking to undermine my excellent relations with the Fuhrer. Ernst Rohm, Rippentrop, especially Rippentrop, Alfred Rosenberg, Himmler even. They've all at times tried to point sneeringly at my foot. I've even had to resort to claiming that my disability is the result of action during the

Great War. Which is feasible as I was 16 when the war began in 1914.

HELMUT: Jokey Gobbler was very lonely and unhappy when he was a little boy. None of the other boys wanted to play with him because he couldn't run and jump like them. And they teased him because of his funny leg and his funny head....

SIEGFRIED: *(impatiently)* Yes, yes. We know all this. Lets move the story along.

BRUNHILDE: I don't know all this. I'm new, remember.

HELMUT: Yes, Brunhilde is new, remember!

SIEGFRIED: *(shrugs)* Suit yourself. You're wasting your turn going over old ground.

HELMUT: The Liar vowed that if no one was going to like him because of the way he looked he would make them like or fear him because he was the cleverest. He read books. Lots and lots of books, on everything. And he rose quickly to the top of the class in everything.

EVERYONE: Liar! Liar! Liar! Pants on Fire!

GOEBBELS: Its true. I have the school reports. Latin, geography, German, mathematics, literature, art, music. I loved playing the piano and I had a particular flair for the theatre. I wrote Gothic tragedies and I was brilliant at acting, if I may be so bold. I was in all the school plays, playing the leads. When I was performing on stage my disability paled into insignificance beside my acting talent. Moments of bliss and adrenalin that enabled me to think I was a God and forget that I was a deformed monster. But those moments were ultimately few and far between. The anguish never went away and I was forever plaguing the local parish priest with questions "Why has God made me this way, so that people would laugh and mock me?" Why did I have to feel hatred when I wanted and needed to feel love? I blamed God for everything, though I often didn't believe he was there. And yet I still placed all my hopes in him. for only God could enable me some day to find recognition and love.

SIEGFRIED: Self-pitying jerk!

GOEBBELS: When I was 13, I decided to study theology in the hope that one day I, too, can sing - "I have found Him whom my soul loveth."

HEIDE: Song of Solomon. Chapter 3. Verse 4.

GOEBBELS: But then I met Lene Krage. The most beautiful girl in town. But not the most intelligent. When we first kissed I was the happiest man in the world. I could not believe that a poor cripple like me had kissed this most beautiful girl. I craved her body while she admired me for my intelligence.

SIEGFRIED: Oh Joe, how unworthy I am compared to you. Yes, you deserved to be worshipped. I could fall into idolatory.

GOEBBELS: Yes. I found her very disturbing. I also had problems with the dark longings, disgusting animal instincts that would shake and squeeze my loins. I felt despicable, demonic. But I lost the struggle against these Satanic urges behind some bushes with Lene in Kaiser Park in 1917. With my virginity gone I decided not to study theology at university but medicine - until my teacher talked me

	into settling on classical philology, German literature and history.
HELMUT:	When the Big War came, Jokey tried to join the game of soldiers, but they wouldn't have him.
SIEGFRIED:	"I'm sorry, old bean but we don't take on cripples - we have fun making our own.
GOEBBELS:	So I continued my studies, had a fabulous affair with a rich, beautiful, aristocratic, intelligent woman called Anka. She was the truest love in my life. Except for the Fuhrer, of course. I got my doctorate in 1921, tried to be a great poet which I was convinced I was destined to be. One of those exceptional human beings whom God had equipped with a special gift, probably because He had so marked my body. Although I had rejected Catholicism and recognised finally that the gap between Christian promises and harsh reality was unbridgeable, I still believed God to be pivotal to fraternity, equality and justice. My vision of socialism was that of Dostoyevski and Tolstoy. I saw God as the great integrator, the synthesising personality of the entire people. If I could find that quality in one man, I will follow him to the end of time.
HEIDE:	Unfortunately for the world he did find the Man who he believed was the Messiah. First he heard about the Bad Man, then he wrote about him, appointing himself as the Bad Man's John the Baptist....
GOEBBELS:	Hitler, oh Hitler my Leader. You who thinks exactly like me, who has spoken after my own heart. You gave a name to the suffering of an entire generation who were yearning

for real men, for meaningful tasks. What you uttered is the catechism of a new political credo amid the desperation of a collapsing, godless world. You did not fall silent. A god gave you strength to voice our suffering. You formulated our torment in redemptive words, formed statements of confidence in the coming miracle.

Scene 9

HEIDE: Then, at last, the Liar met him. The Bad Man was also dying to meet him. He just loved the things Jokey Gobbler wrote about him. And they became blood-brothers - using everybody else's but their own.

HITLER (KARL): So you agree with everything I believe, to be true? Why the War was lost. The Cause of the Decline of Western Civilisation. My racial theories, that the Jew is the root of all evil, the Jew is the Anti-Christ, the Jew is the satanic power behind capitalism and international Marxism?

GOEBBELS: Oh indubitably! One hundred percent! (*turns to audience*) Well, not entirely. I did have difficulties with the Boss' view that the Slavs were sub-human, inferior. You can't think that when you've read Dostoyevski, Chekhov, Tolstoy and Lenin. It would be a shame to march on Russia - and yet when I look into those big blue eyes. Like stars, and feel his hero's hand press mine like an old friend, all my doubts fall away. This man has everything it takes to be king. He is the natural born tribune of the people. The Coming Dictator. My friend and master, bonded to the very end with a shared glorious

vision.   *(turns back to HITLER)* I thought
your chapter on the art of propaganda
particularly illuminating, if I may say so.

HITLER (KARL): Well, my in depth analysis of our disastrous
war has made me realise that the Tommies
are not just ferocious fighters but also
brilliant at propaganda. Whereas we were
complete crap. I fervently believe that the
Propaganda War is what cost us the war.
Apart from being stabbed in the back by our
own Bolshevik Jewry, of course. No - we
have a lot to learn from the English!

*(HITLER / Karl puts a paternalistic hand on GOEBBEL's
shoulder and together they walk stage right)*

HITLER (KARL): How is your foot? It must be very hard for
you?

GOEBBELS: No, no. Its no bother....

HITLER (KARL): Yes but it must cause you a lot of pain?
You're the Suffering in Silence type, I can
tell.

GOEBBELS: No really. I... barely notice... Its nothing.

HITLER (KARL): I must say I admire your courage. I really
do. Born with it, were you?

GOEBBELS: *(horrified)* Eh ... No. No, it was an accident...
er...my mother -

(The Odd Couple exit, so we hear no more)

HEIDE: And so Jokey Gobbler continued to lie his
way to the top, and became Mr. Big of
Berlin.

HELMUT: Even though he was really small.

HEIDE:	Where he helped his Lord and King, the Bad Man launch his war against the Jews, the World and us.
HELMUT:	Even though he was one of us.

Scene 10

(SPOTTGEBURT is conferring with DR. DRECK / Eva and DR. TODT / Fritz. They are interrupted by an obviously distraught DR. EWALD)

EWALD:	It's official now, is it? The euthanasia project has been extended from children to adults? I suppose you're satisfied now! Pleased are you? Now that the Fuhrer has personally given the green light to create your brave new world. I believe the decree was actually written on his own private stationery! My, my, how honoured you are!
SPOTTGEBURT:	Dr. Ewald, it is not a question of being "satisfied", "pleased" or "honoured". We are at war. Our nation is fighting for its very existence. And as the Fuhrer rightly said - it is intolerable that the best, the flower of our youth must lose its life at the front in order that feeble-minded and irresponsible asocial elements can have secure existence in sanatoriums and asylums.
EWALD:	A war that is completely and utterly pointless. The man is a total nutter. He should be certified. HE belongs in here, not those poor wretches -
SPOTTGEBURT:	Herr Doktor Ewald! Stop this immediately. You bloody fool. You're lucky you have friends here. You are also lucky you have very good friends in high places. However,

your private consultancy to Hermann
Goering won't always save you from the
concentration camps, if you persist in making
public such treasonable thoughts. Keep them
private - and live!

EWALD: Listen, I AM A DOCTOR! And I swore an
oath to heal and save life. Human life. Not
obsolete machinery. Not lame horses and
cows. But humans like me. And I tell you,
Herr DOKTOR, we commit an act of
extraordinary arrogance if we take it upon
ourselves to put an end to a human life
simply because we lack the imaginative skills
to grasp the meaning and value of that life.

SPOTTGEBURT: My dear Gottfried, I didn't know you were
such an incurable romantic. You know its no
longer healthy to be "incurable".

EWALD: Jesus, I never thought you'd stoop so low
as....

SPOTTGEBURT: Doktor Ewald, this insubordinancy has gone
quite far enough. I am not interested in the
slightest what you believe. I order you to take
these T4 questionnaires back to your asylum
and have them filled in.

EWALD: Go to hell.

SPOTTGEBURT: If you don't fill them in, then some one else
will. And I can assure you their net will have
far smaller holes than yours.

*(EWALD hesitates then finally gives in and takes a
bundle and examples the forms)*

EWALD: What does this "T - 4" mean, anyway?

EVA: The T-4 program is so named because the
organisation, the Reich Work Group of
Sanatoriums and Nursing Homes, which has

been specially set up to run it, has its headquarters at the Chancellery at Tiergarten 4. These questionnaires have been devised by top psychiatrists and medical administrators and are being issued via the Health Ministry to all psychiatric institutions, hospitals and homes for disabled and other chronic patients, throughout the Reich.

FRITZ: They have been designed to give the impression that a major statistical survey is being carried for administrative and scientific purposes, focusing on budgets, number of beds, number of doctors and nurses. That sort of thing.

EVA: But embedded within these spurious questions are others that ask for precise descriptions of the working ability of inmates and which require you to define the patients according to one of the 4 categories.

FRITZ: One - Specified diseases rendering adults unemployable or only employable in simple mechanical work, such as schizophrenia, epilepsy, senile diseases, therapy-resistant paralysis, syphilitic sequelae, feeble-mindedness from any cause, encephalitis, Huntingdon's Chorea and other neurological conditions of a terminal nature.

EVA: If a patient is so defined -

SPOTTGEBURT: He must die.

FRITZ: Two - Patients who have been continually institutionalised for at least 5 years.

EVA: If a patient is so defined -

SPOTTGEBURT: He must die.

EWALD: If one of my patients has been in continuous
                care for more than 5 years, HE MUST DIE?

EVA: Yes.

FRITZ: Three - Custodial criminally insane.

EVA: If a patient is so defined -

SPOTTGEBURT: He must die.

FRITZ: Four - Not German or kindred blood, giving
                race and nationality.

EVA: If a pa -

EWALD: (interrupts) If a patient is so defined, he must
                die. Yeah, I think I get the picture.

EVA: The completed questionnaires will be
                processed and checked by experts who will
                give final authorization to the Death
                Decisions.

FRITZ: Transport lists will then be sent to hospitals
                with names of patients who are to be
                transported to one of six principle special
                centres of convalescence.

SPOTTGEBURT: In reality - killing centres, specially
                designed to facilitate 30 or more killings an
                hour, complete with cremation ovens.

FRITZ: The six main centres are Hartheim,
                Sonnenstein, Grafeneck, Bernburg,
                Brandenburg and Hadamar.

EVA: Transportation will be by special buses with
                blacked out windows, run by the "Common
                Welfare Ambulance Service Ltd" which has
                been specifically created for this job.

SPOTTGEBURT: Naturally, the people manning the buses will
                not be anyone from the medical fraternity.

They will be SS personnel wearing white uniforms or white coats, masquerading as doctors, nurses or medical attendants. They will give instructions that patients be accompanied by case histories, personal and valuable possessions, and will carry special permits to pass through checkpoints unhindered and unchallenged.

EWALD: *(to FRITZ)* And you don't find this objectionable and grotesque?

(FRITZ refuses to comment)

EWALD: *(to EVA)* What about you? You're a woman.

(EVA is silent)

SPOTTGEBURT: Are you telling me you don't agree with euthanasia under any circumstances?

EWALD: Oh, as a doctor I have aided and abetted voluntary euthanasia. Tell me what doctor hasn't! When confronted with a patient with terminal cancer who literally begs me to hasten their death. Certainly. Every sensible doctor approves of some euthanasia. And I would certainly kill in defence of my nation. I would also approve the elimination of serious criminals and common vermin. But I cannot continue in a profession whose daily business is to eliminate a sick person because of his sickness, when he or his relations have come to me, trusting and looking for help.

SPOTTGEBURT: But my dear Gottfried, once you accept some euthanasia - albeit voluntary - aren't you on the slippery slope?

EWALD: Don't "my dear Gottfried" me. That's not what's at issue here. I am warning you that fear and distrust will be rampant towards us, doctors, because people will know that admission to a mental hospital or special institution can lead to death. Not only would medical care for the entire population suffer, but the medical profession would lose its general standing and people would associate us with everything that is sinister, monstrous and terrible.

(EWALD marches right up to SPOTTGEBURT, nose to nose, eye to eye)

EWALD:　　　*(hisses)* No. On principle. I will not lend my hand to exterminate in this way patients entrusted to me. You can take these questionnaires and stuff them in those ovens you so obviously relish.

(EWALD throws the bundle of forms into SPOTTGEBURT's face and storms off stage)

(FRITZ and SPOTTGEBURT exit, leaving EVA to pick up the papers. GOEBBELS enters, sees her and comes up behind her, gooses her and takes her in his arms. They passionately embrace, kissing like there's no tomorrow, with their hands feverishly groping. Suddenly, GOEBBELS stops and pushes EVA away.)

GOEBBELS:　　*(to the audience)* Meet Else, one of my earlier flames. A nice school-teacher, who has compassion for me, and admires my intellect. Huh! But she finds my clubbed foot repulsive and wonders whether I am the right man to father her children. Also darling Else tries to conceal our relationship from the neighbours. This of course, I hate and I quarrel with her constantly.

(GOEBBELS grabs ELSE / Eva, and they kiss each other with even greater passion and fury, almost to the point of

*violence. Again GOEBBELS stops suddenly and pushes
ELSE / Eva from him)*

GOEBBELS: *(to the audience)* Have you ever wondered
why I hated the Jews so much? I didn't
always. I mean, like everyone else I use to
think they were a bloody nuisance. But wipe
them out? Totally remove them from the face
of the earth? No. I did not want that. That
would have been barbaric. Evil. And we
Germans are a civilized, cultured people.
Racial genocide has never been our style. So
what changed? Well, certain philosophical
writers made me re-evaluate my somewhat
liberal position, Spengler, for example. He
argued very persuasively that the Jew was the
greatest threat to Mankind. And that if we
were to survive as a civilized species, the Jew
must be ruthlessly exterminated, as you
would with any vermin. But that's not the
whole story of why I now so hate the Jews.
Actually, to be honest, the Jews are just a
convenient focus for this burning need I
have, to hate. I want to be able to hate. To be
a real human you have to both love and hate.
And I hate all those who rob me of my right
to hate because God gave it to me... Oh, I can
hate, and I don't want to forget how.... Oh,
how wonderful it is to be able to hate. And...
to have someone to hate. And if I can't hate
the Jews, who else can I hate? Someone has
to pay for the way I've been treated all my
life. Despised, mocked, treated as inferior, as
if I was a fucking Jew.

ELSE: I wish you would stop all this talk of Jews.

GOEBBELS: Why?

ELSE: Well, if you must know - my mother is
                    Jewish.

GOEBBELS: What?

ELSE: You heard. So stop being so boorish about
                    Jews.

GOEBBELS: WHAT?

ELSE: Look on the bright side. You are half a man.
                    And I am half a Jew. Obviously we were
                    made for each other.

GOEBBELS: *(screams)* **WHAT ?**

*(He explodes with fury, storms over to ELSE and
viciously kicks her in the stomach. He then frog marches
her off stage)*

Scene 11

*(Up stage The Story Tellers have gathered once again.
Down stage FRITZ and BRUNHILDE are working a
chore together)*

FRITZ: Are you married?

BRUNHILDE: Do I look married? Do I have time to be
                    married?

FRITZ: Well, I don't know. You're not unattractive,
                    you've got a good figure - despite -

(BRUNHILDE turns angrily on FRITZ)

BRUNHILDE: Despite what?

FRITZ: Don't get me wrong. Look, I'm trying to pay
                    you a compliment. I was just wondering, you
                    know - may be sometime one evening. Go
                    for a drink or something. What do you say?

BRUNHILDE:	I wouldn't go with you if you was the last man on earth!
FRITZ:	Jesus, you're touchy. I'm just trying to be sociable. I get lonely too, you know. *(looks over his shoulder at the patients)* Hanging around with them is not going to do you much good. Not in the long run.
BRUNHILDE:	Yes, you keeping hinting at something. What the hell are you driving at?
FRITZ:	I wish I knew. I merely have a feeling that its not advisable for you to spend so much time with them. People might start thinking you're an inmate, then you'll be glad to have a friend in me. Please, believe me. Your life might depend on it.

(FRITZ exits. BRUNHILDE joins the GANG)

SIEGFRIED:	What does old Fritz want?
BRUNHILDE:	Oh, just trying to chat me up.
SIEGFRIED:	Yeah? Fancy him, do you?
BRUNHILDE:	Well, he has got a nice bum.
SIEGFRIED:	Huh!
HEIDE:	Where were we?
BRUNHILDE:	It's my turn, I think.
HELMUT:	Yeah! It's Brunhilde's turn. Hooray!
BRUNHILDE:	Right. Now, not everyone in the land loved the Bad Man and agreed with what he was doing. A few members of the aristocracy and some generals in the Army High Command quickly realised they had made a huge mistake helping to crown this evil man King. They arrogantly believed that this seemingly

insignificant little man was stupid and could be controlled by them. They foolishly thought that because their families had been running the country for hundred of years they were the only people with brains. However, once it became obvious to some of them that the Bad Man was serious about his crazy ideas and was going to plunge the nation into another ghastly war, they started a plot to get rid of him. One of their ideas was to kidnap him and have psychiatrists declare him insane....

SIEGFRIED: Good God no! We might have had him in with us!

BRUNHILDE: Anyway they quickly gave up on that plan and decided that only the military was capable of removing him, and so they started to look for the most respected and idealistic man among them who could lead and organise a military coup. Soon, they found him. And that man was....

(Eva steps forward as NINA VON STAUFFENBERG)

NINA: My husband - Claus Philipp Count Schenk von Stauffenberg, born 1907, aristocrat and descended from a long line of illustrious military commanders.

HELMUT: Our Hero?

BRUNHILDE: Yes our Hero. A brave soldier who loved music, gaiety and horses. He especially loved horses. He would ride them all day.

HELMUT: *(disappointed)* He wasn't one of us, then.

BRUNHILDE: Well... er...

HELMUT: Say yes. Please!

BRUNHILDE:	Er... Oh alright. But not straight away. First he was like I was before the bomb hit my hospital.
HEIDE:	If he had begun like us, he couldn't have joined the army and become our hero.
SIEGFRIED:	Bullshit! First, soldiers are not the only heroes, and secondly, I don't see why we can't be heroes too.
HELMUT:	Be quiet, Siegfried! It's still Brunhilde's go.
SIEGFRIED:	Sorry, Bru.
BRUNHILDE:	Bru?
SIEGFRIED:	Brunhilde.
BRUNHILDE:	Hmmm. Anyway, as a schoolboy Our Hero loved to act and he had two favourite speeches. One was the speech by Brutus in Shakespeare's "Julius Caesar".

Scene 12

(CLAUS / Ewald / Luke wearing an artificial arm at the back of the stage, back-lit so as to be in silhouette)

CLAUS:	"It must be by his death. The abuse of greatness is when it disjoins remorse from power, think him as a serpent's egg which, hatched, would as his kind, grow mischievous and kill him."
BRUNHILDE:	And his second was in Schiller's "Wilhelm Tell" -
CLAUS:	"There is a limit to a tyrant's might! When the oppressed can find no justice from here below, when the burden becomes intolerable, then he will summon the courage to reach up

to the heavens themselves and grasp those eternal rights which are as unchanged and indestructible as the stars in the sky. We must defend the highest virtues against all and every power."

NINA: Claus von Stauffenberg was immensely proud of his aristocratic and military forebears and was eager to become an officer in the 7th Banberg Cavalry regiment. And by 1936 he was a first-rate horseman and rode with the Hanover Cavalry team which won the Berlin Olympics. He was never a true supporter of the Nazis but he had to join the party in order to further his career. By 1938 Claus had joined the General Staff which was headed by General Beck who thoroughly disapproved of Hitler's rapid expansion and mechanisation of the military and was fighting a losing battle to keep the army un-Nazified. And it was then that Claus started to get involved in plots against Hitler.

(CLAUS steps up to NINA)

CLAUS: Nina, would you believe I have just come from a secret meeting with Generals Beck, Witzleben and Hoepner in which it was discussed that should this Munich crisis go badly and war breaks out over Czechoslovakia we will employ our regiments against Hitler and arrest him, Goering, Himmler, Goebbels, the whole blasted lot.

NINA: Claus, I shouldn't be hearing this and I don't want to. Already people are expecting too much of you. You told me last week that your uncle Count von Uxkull, and the deputy police president of Berlin, Count

Schulanberg had approached you to put an end to this shameful government. Well, I'm sorry but they are complete idiots! How can you? You are a mere cavalry officer, 31 years old and barely a Captain.

CLAUS: I know, Nina, I know. But Schulenberg believes that I could act if I was to get myself appointed adjutant to Brauchitsch, the Army Commander-in-Chief.

NINA: But, darling, is it really that simple? Since when were we living in a fairy story?

BRUNHILDE: Well, it was that easy for Our Hero to rise rapidly to a powerful position, what with his family connections, old boys' network and the growing military build-up for war.

Scene 13

(SPOTTGEBURT is filling in a form. FRITZ is changing bed-linen up stage)

SPOTTGEBURT: Fritz, how long has that idiot Helmut been an inmate here?

FRITZ: Helmut? Nearly 3 years, Herr Doktor.

SPOTTGEBURT: Only 3 years. Would you say he was employable?

FRITZ: Employable? Good heavens no. The poor lad can barely tie his own shoe laces!

SPOTTGEBURT: Good, good.

(SPOTTGEBURT signs the form and puts it on another pile)

BRUNHILDE: Despite his hatred for the Bad Man when the war finally started, Our Hero did his duty when called and actually quite enjoyed himself.

CLAUS: You can't help feel invigorated to see Germany at last flex its muscles - no matter what your persuasion. You wouldn't be human, you wouldn't be German. I'm not a Nazi but I am a soldier and a patriot and I have to confess despite my misgivings these astonishing victories of ours on these hot days have been exciting.

SIEGFRIED: I thought the Generals were going to rebel if there was war?

BRUNHILDE: I'm afraid they bottled out. Besides the Bad Man sacked the Top General before the fighting began.

SPOTTGEBURT: What about Heide?

FRITZ: Now she's very bright. Very learned. The books she's read. Once you get past that awful spastic speech sound of hers, you realise she's not as dumb as she looks.

SPOTTGEBURT: I see. And who has wasted money giving her an education? How long has she been institutionalised?

FRITZ: Oooh, a good few years, I should think.

SPOTTGEBURT: More than five years?

FRITZ: Oh yes, Herr Doktor, certainly more than 5 years!

(SPOTTGEBURT puts another form on top of a growing pile)

CLAUS: We've been at war now for nearly a year and we have reached Paris, but I do think his triumphal parade through the city's streets rather vulgar. Talk about rubbing the French noses in it. Who does the Fuhrer think he is - some oriental emperor? What I find horrifying is the possibility that we have a conqueror who thinks he is the reincarnation of Frederick the Great, or worse. Because he is completely lacking in sentiment and a sense of proportion. I fear he will become our nation's doom.

SIEGFRIED: So what do you propose?

CLAUS: If this Fuhrer of ours is incapable of mastering this lust for power and his perverse craving for barbaric exhibitionism....

SIEGFRIED: ...he should be removed?

CLAUS: Yes. But we should be serious this time.

SIEGFRIED: Killed, you mean?

CLAUS: Good God no. I'm a soldier and I believe soldiering is or should be an honourable profession. I couldn't possibly countenance the murder of our leader. To do so would be to sink to his depraved level.

SIEGFRIED: Perhaps something will change your mind. Lets hope it will not be too late in its coming.

SPOTTGEBURT: And Siegfried?

FRITZ: That little shit-stirrer! Sorry sir. Nah he's alright really. If he could get rid of that chip on his shoulder, he could be quite human.

SPOTTGEBURT: I'm not asking for an attitude rating. How long has he been an inmate?

FRITZ: All his life. He was dumped here the moment he was born. His mother nearly committed suicide when she saw the state of him. I reckon he must have broken every bone in his body coming out of her.

SPOTTGEBURT: Jolly good. Another 5 year category. That makes it 153. I think we are going to need about ten transportations.

BRUNHILDE: No matter how much the Hero tried, he could not persuade all the top generals to co-operate in his plans to capture the Bad Man. Most of them were in full sympathy with his motives but none of them would take the initiative, be responsible. They all wanted superior orders. And as one of them said -

FRITZ: "....the only man who can order me to act against the Fuhrer is the Fuhrer"

BRUNHILDE: - In the end Our Hero got so disillusioned he asked to be sent to the Front...

HELMUT: And then he became one of us?

BRUNHILDE: Yes.

HELMUT: Hooray!

BRUNHILDE: His army car got shot up by low flying enemy aircraft and he was so badly wounded he had to lose an arm....

HELMUT: Just like Doktor Ewald?

BRUNHILDE: Yes but he also lost an eye and 2 fingers from his other hand.

HELMUT: Yippee! Now he's one of us, he can kill the Bad Man.

Scene 14

(FRITZ enters with suitcases)

FRITZ: Alright you vegetables, get all your things together, clothes, valuables, the lot. You've got to pack your bags.

BRUNHILDE: What? Where are they going? Nobody told me.

FRITZ: Listen sweetheart, I've only just found out, so why should anyone tell you! Come on, all of you, we're going on a nice little journey.

SIEGFRIED: What now?

FRITZ: The ambulances will be here in an hour. That's right, pack your chess set.

HELMUT: Where are we going?

FRITZ: A nice little home. In the country.

BRUNHILDE: Where, Fritz? WHERE?

FRITZ: *(whispers)* How the hell should I know?

BRUNHILDE: You know more than you're letting on.

FRITZ: I don't, honest. They won't tell me a thing.

HEIDE: So why is there is this smell of death about you?

FRITZ: *(almost hysterical)* Don't be daft!

(BRUNHILDE grabs FRITZ and forces him to the side, out of earshot)

BRUNHILDE: Fritz, something has spooked you.

FRITZ: Look, I don't know. It's just that I've got a bad feeling about this.

BRUNHILDE: I'm going to collect my things.

(BRUNHILDE runs off stage)

FRITZ: **BRUNHILDE ! NO! NO! NO!**

ACT II

Scene 1

(Present day - The hotel room at the Convention centre)

GEORGE: We, disabled people, especially those of us
with congenital disabilities, should refuse to
take part in any genetic tests. We should not
co-operate in any way with the Human
Genome Research Project. Not just because
we will be giving ammunition to employers
more reason, more excuses not to employ us
- not just because anyone with so-called
hereditary diseases will become a part of an
uninsurable underclass, but also because we
should be in the vanguard of resisting this
international co-ordinated attempt to improve
the race which is presented under the guise of
"health" policy. Sisters and brothers, doesn't
this sound horribly familiar to you. It is no
accident that we should be holding this
conference in Berlin in a now United
Germany. Medicine once again, as it was
during the Third Reich, is becoming the
regime of eugenic management, and with so-
called gene therapy - a sinister euphemism if
ever there was one - the instrument for the
manipulation of genes. As Gene Technology
and the concomitant Gene Ethos takes hold
of our society, people are going to be told
that if they know that certain genes cause
disease, and can be tested for them, then it
would be irresponsible to leave it to chance,
and it would be irresponsible and cruel to
even consider bringing a disabled child into

85

the world.

As a person born with a disability I find these arguments deeply offensive and very, very frightening. When I hear expressions like "healthy genetic endowment" I feel scared. When I hear "pre-nuptial counselling" I feel scared. When I hear "pre-natal screening" I feel despised and scared. When I hear gene therapy on either the foetus or child, I feel despised, useless and scared.

We disabled people of today are luckier than the disabled people of Germany's Third Reich, we have the past to warn us of the future. We must learn from that history and fight - Fight hard, and if necessary Fight Bloody!

JONAH: Bloody brilliant! You're going to knock their bloody socks off with that tomorrow. Well, I must say, you certainly seem to have recovered from your hypnosis trip down memory lane.

GEORGE: *(smiles)* Jonah, you shit, I'll take your compliment but I won't take your mocking. I never want to go through that again. But it was amazing. I completely re-lived that era. Everything. It was so real. You know something, none of us have the slightest idea of what's stored in here. *(taps his head)* I'm beginning to suspect that our minds are time-machines. Its just a question of discovering the methods of access and control.

Regression hypnosis could be one of the keys for unlocking this Doctor Who TARDIS lurking in these bonces. I am convinced in the future we will know how to let our minds travel freely through time and space. Maybe our genes are the data banks holding

	information on every event, every memory of history. Which would be another good reason for stopping the gene engineers.
JONAH:	Bloody hell, George, if its not one weird notion, it's another! So you no longer think you're the reincarnation of Hitler?
GEORGE:	No I don't. Or Himmler. When I think about it, my life just hasn't been bad enough to be any kind of punishment for those evil bastards. No, if I was any of them I was probably the Good Doktor Goebbels, since he completely failed to learn anything from that existence as a mildly disabled person. But even that I'm not taking seriously. Lately I've been questioning all my previous ideas on the transmigration of souls and the recycling of spiritual waste. And yet the notion of Eternal Damnation is just too silly, childish and short-sighted. And ultimately a cosmic burden. I mean, how can a universe grow and evolve into a perfect One-ness of Being when it contains such an infinite bottleneck of the Damned!
JONAH:	Oh yeah Man! Wow! Wicked! Sound! Far out! You aged Hippy you! I notice you still can't escape the idea of disability of being some kind of punishment, though. Despite all your consciousness raising.
GEORGE:	Yeah I know. Pathetic isn't it! A wretched demented product of society's brainwashing. That's me.
JONAH:	Oh I wouldn't go that far. Demented yes, but wretched? Hello, what's this?

(JONAH who had been rifling around GEORGE's papers and books, discovers a black book under some clothes)

JONAH: Bloody hell! I don't believe it! Where the
                hell did you get a hold of this?

GEORGE: SHIT! Put it back!

JONAH: This is supposed to be banned.

GEORGE: I know. So put it back.

*(JONAH doesn't. Instead he sits on the bed and goes
through it)*

JONAH: Well I never - "The Anarchist Cook Book"!
                Where did you get it?

GEORGE: A friend of a friend who has a friend....

JONAH: ...Who also has a friend... I know. Look at
                this - recipes on how to make L.S.D.!
                Fantastic! Can I make a photo-copy?

GEORGE: No you bloody can't. Put the fucker back.

JONAH: Come on - just the L.S.D. recipes. Please.
                Pretty please.

GEORGE: There's a recipe there on how to make
                hallucinogens from banana skins.

JONAH: Where? Ah so! The secret is out! Now I
                know why you so bananas!

GEORGE: But you've got to eat 15 bananas first.

*(Stage left, a SMALL BLUE SPOT OF LIGHT starts to
grow)*

JONAH: Shit!

*(The Blue Spot reveals BRUNHILDE staring at
GEORGE)*

GEORGE: Exactly.

*(GEORGE notices BRUNHILDE, looks at JONAH and
realises he alone sees her)*

88

JONAH: It's all probably lies anyway. I've heard that
            this book was cooked up by the C.I.A., and
            not by genuine revolutionary anarchists. That
            some of the recipes are very dodgy and
            aimed to backfire and kill or damage the
            anarchist chef.

GEORGE: Yeah, and I've also heard that that is a piece
            of disinformation put out by the C.I.A. in an
            attempt to discredit it's authentic subversive
            content, so as to discourage any serious
            application.

JONAH: A double-double bluff, huh! Dead clever,
            these damn Yankees! What's true and what's
            false? But are you prepared to take the risk
            and experiment with these recipes. I mean,
            shit, there's a chapter here on explosives and
            booby-traps!

            *(Another BLUE SPOT OF LIGHT reveals HEIDE and
            HELMUT)*

GEORGE: Jonah, please put the bloody book away.

            *(GEORGE is even more dumbfounded when he notices
            HEIDE and HELMUT)*

JONAH: "How to make nitro-glycerine" - "How to
            make mercury fulminate" - "How to make
            blasting gelatine"

GEORGE: Jonah, please.

JONAH;   "Formulas for gelatine dynamites" - "How to
            make TNT". Someone has underlined these
            paragraphs. "Probably the most important
            explosive compound in use today is TNT -
            Trinitrotoluene - This and other very similar
            types of high explosives are all used by the
            military, because of their fantastic power -
            about 2.25 million pounds per square inch,

and their great stability"....Jesus!...
"Preparation of TNT... One. Take two
beakers. In the first prepare a solution of 76
percent Sulphuric acid, 23 percent Nitric
acid, and 1 percent water. In the other
beaker...." -

(JONAH continues reading to himself)

JONAH: Wow, this is bloody dynamite!

GEORGE: No. TNT. Now put the book down!

*(JONAH does and piles clothes on top of it, and looks
searchingly at GEORGE's face)*

JONAH: George. What's going on? What are you
               planning?

GEORGE: Nothing. Its just a silly little book. Probably,
               as you say, written by the C.I.A. for crazed
               American right wing survivalists, and Eco-
               terrorists.

JONAH: Do you know what the average life
               expectancy of an Amateur Bomber is? As
               short as the longest fuse.

*(HELMUT and HEIDE dance around JONAH, pulling
faces. JONAH, however is completely oblivious of them)*

(LUKE enters)

LUKE: Hi guys. Whose volunteering to go on picket
               duty outside the Schneider Genetic Research
               Institute?

JONAH: No good asking George, he probably thinks
               it's a waste of time! I expect he'd rather blow
               the place up.

GEORGE: No I don't think pickets are a waste of time.
               There are many ways to skin a cat.

JONAH: Including blowing poor Moggy to bits. I
                wouldn't let your Animal Liberation pals
                hear you say that!

*(HELMUT does a silent explosion mime. GEORGE
laughs)*

GEORGE: Yeah, you're right. Inappropriate analogy.
                But you know what I mean. In any struggle
                there has to be a multi-pronged approach.
                The way of the Moderate in tandem with the
                radical tactics of the Militant, to feed off each
                other. That way the pressure is kept up on the
                establishment bastards.

JONAH: So you do believe there is a place for
                violence? For bombs and things?

GEORGE: You have to fight ruthlessness with
                ruthlessness. Force with force. Do you think
                Gandhi could have won against Hitler. He
                would have just been the first to die in a
                concentration camp, with his hunger strike.
                The early Gandhi tactics failed to get rid of
                Apartheid in South Africa. And the I.R.A.
                hunger strikes in the early Eighties were
                cynically viewed by Thatcher as own goals.
                No. Sometimes violence is the most -

*(GEORGE stops in mid sentence as he sees BRUNHILDE
signal him to keep silent)*

JONAH: Yes? Sometimes violence is what?

GEORGE: Has it suddenly got cold in here?

(JONAH and LUKE look at each other)

JONAH: No. What do you mean?

GEORGE: I don't know. I just suddenly feel all shivery.

LUKE: Oh dear, George is going to have one of his
                   funny turns.

JONAH: Are you alright, mate?

GEORGE: I think I need a lie-down. That hypnotism
                   stuff has taken more out of me than I realise.

JONAH: Alright mate, you have a lie-down. Come on
                   Luke. I'll go on picket duty with you. See
                   you George. Take it easy.

LUKE: George, I'm really sorry. I didn't realise how
                   little I knew.

GEORGE: It's okay, Luke. There were other forces at
                   work. You didn't stand a chance. Go on, piss
                   off.

*(grinning, JONAH and LUKE exit, giving GEORGE the
V-sign)*

*(BRUNHILDE, HELMUT and HEIDE approach
GEORGE. They help him to undress and change into the
inmate's pyjamas.* **SIEGFRIED has returned***)*

Scene 2

BRUNHILDE: *(to the audience)* I was allowed to travel with
                   my patients, my friends, my Heide, Siegfried
                   and my Helmut. The escort were actually
                   quite decent about it. They said that if my
                   accompanying the patients would make them
                   feel less anxious, "more manageable" - their
                   words, put their worried little minds at rest,
                   then of course, I should come.
                   It was a strange journey, not knowing where
                   we were going. Windows blacked out, so we

couldn't see out. And we packed like
sardines and it was a stiflingly hot day! I
could barely breath. But the escort had
packed us a nice lunch, and encouraged the
patients to sing cheerful songs to while away
the long hours of driving. In fact it took
several days to get to our ultimate
destination, so we had two stop-over nights
at various sanatoriums on the way. It was all
very mysterious. We would arrive at a
particular institution at the dead of night,
taken to a special wing sealed off from the
rest of the hospital. We would be ordered to
eat and go to bed. Me, included. No matter
how much I tried - I couldn't get any info.
Then at the crack of dawn we would be off
again. I have to say, I started to feel uneasy.
Our escort - or guards, for that's what they
seem to be - were becoming less friendly as
we got further from Berlin. When I'd try to
look at them in the eyes, they would quickly
glance away. If I smiled at them, they would
stare back, stoney-faced. By the end of the
second day of travelling I could feel a twisted
knot growing in my guts. Something was
definitely wrong. When we got to our final
destination there was an almighty furore.
Would you believe it, we weren't expected!
Someone had given our driver and escort the
wrong instructions. We'd been sent hundreds
of miles to the wrong place! Well, we
couldn't go all the way back, but neither
could we stay - not at that time - so we were
sent on ten miles to a transit institution in the
city of Limburg, and there we stayed for a
few weeks while the bureaucracy was being
disentangled. I knew we were in Limberg
because since we would be staying over for a

while, the escort didn't boss us about so much, and as a member of staff, I occasionally had to go into town. And it was on these visits that I began , at last, to get inklings of the horrible, horrible truth.

(The Story Tellers gather for another round)

SIEGFRIED: One of the jobs Jokey Gobbler liked most in his role of Chief Lie-Maker, was running the nation's film production industry. First of all, he was a complete film-buff. He would watch all the latest American Hollywood movies, admire and praise them, and then ban them, so that only he and his closest friends could ever watch them. Secondly, his rulership gave him an opportunity to meddle in every aspect of the film making process, from writing, choosing directors, casting to censorship. At any point in the production he could and usually did interfere. His cultural and social life blossomed as famous actors, beautiful film stars and great film-makers hovered around him, hoping to gain his patronage. Without him, they wouldn't have a career.

Scene 3

(COCKTAIL PARTY - FRITZ and KARL looking at GOEBBELS who is overly attentive to EVA)

FRITZ: I see the Reich Minister Josef Goebbels is at his womanising again. I don't know how that limping devil does it!

KARL: Ah there you have it. There's nothing like a cloven hoof to send the ladies wild. The dark satanic looks have great sex appeal.

(They laugh sneeringly)

KARL: No. Actually its much simpler and more
            sordid than that. It's common gossip that the
            only way a would-be starlet can hope for an
            acting contract is show herself amenable to
            our Minister's voracious sexual appetites. It
            all goes on behind closed doors at the
            Ministry - so I'm told.

FRITZ: Does the Fuhrer know?

KARL: Well, apparently the SS have been keeping a
            secret dossier on our Propaganda Minister's
            amorous adventures. Himmler tells me that
            he has had innumerable complaints from
            women about his sexual abuse and
            harassment. He has had to have quiet words
            with the Fuhrer. Our little Doktor Goebbels
            has become a bit of an open scandal.
            Himmler sees him as National Socialism's
            greatest moral burden and probably the most
            hated man in Germany.

FRITZ: *(laughs)* Aren't we being a bit hypocritical?
            I've certainly dallied and I know you have.
            To be frank, I think we are outraged and hate
            him because he is a damn cripple who is
            having more success than we are.

KARL: No doubt that is what *he* would say.
            Incidentally, did I tell you about Hermann
            Goering's latest little peccadillo.....

(They wander off. GOEBBELS steps forward)

GOEBBELS: Isn't she beautiful! Just perfect for the
            support-role in Frolich's next comedy "The
            Gas - Man". I've promised her the part...and
            er...with no strings attached, if you know
            what I mean. No. She deserves it. Anyway

I've been told to behave myself. I've
promised the Fuhrer......

(GOEBBELS turns and joins KARL and FRITZ)

GOEBBELS: Ah Herr Doktor Brandt.

KARL: Doktor Goebbels.

GOEBBELS: How's the Euthanasia program progressing?

(They drink cocktails)

KARL: I'm glad to say we've solved most of the
teething problems. There are still a few
transportation snarl-ups. We're not always
able to eliminate the pieces within 24 hours
of arrival, which is our aim.

GOEBBELS: Pieces? You call the victims "pieces"?
Interesting. And necessary. Turn the subject
into object, and you can remove empathy and
any danger of identification with those you
have to -

FRITZ: Despatch. We're still looking for the most
efficient method of despatch.

GOEBBELS: Killing.

FRITZ: Yes. We've been experimenting with
shooting, starvation, drugs in food, narcotic
injections and gassings. Gassing with carbon
monoxide looks the most promising.
Although Dr. Brandt, here, fears it is a trifle
un-medical, and wants to run a few more
tests before a final decision is made.

GOEBBELS: *(aside to the audience)* These physicians and
their gassing experiments are causing us a lot
of problems with the evacuation of children
from cities that are being bombed. Mothers
are hearing rumours and are refusing to let

their children be taken. The Fuhrer is very concerned. *(to KARL and FRITZ)* Don't you find all these experiments in death rather gruesome?

KARL: I can see you are not a doctor of science!

GOEBBELS: No, I'm a literary man myself.

KARL: Nonetheless I know you appreciate the vital role we have in rebuilding the German nation. As you are aware the Fuhrer takes a personal interest in every stage of our work. I will probably turn to him for advise when I have to choose between injections or gassings. For the time being we will stay with injections. I feel much more comfortable with the syringe. It may be slower but I admire its aesthetic quality. It has a wonderful, clear, streamline look, it is the most sacred of the physician's instruments and it can deliver a completely painless peaceful death.

GOEBBELS: And it's very phallic looking.

KARL: Doktor Goebbels, you sound like a Freudianist. Surely, you are not a disciple of this Jewish heresy? You, one of our toughest anti-Jew crusaders. *(laughs)* I am shocked.

FRITZ: Wasn't it you who dreamed up that glass-shattering extravaganza - "Crystal Night" you called it.

GOEBBELS: Yes, that was my little baby. The sound of a thousand broken Jewish shop windows! Music to my ears.

KARL: But, Doktor Goebbels, returning to your observation concerning the syringe. You may have a point, for I am reminded of an extraordinary dream I had the other night. I dreamt that after my death I would live in a special place where I would rule, where I would be sent millions upon millions of people to kill personally with phenol injections -

GOEBBELS: Phenol?

KARL: Carbolic acid. Normally we use it in ear drops but it is lethal when injected. It is, by far, my most favoured lethal narcotic. Anyway, it was a wonderful dream. It made me feel good. It is a beautiful exhilarating feeling to have absolute omnipotence. When I awoke the next morning, would you believe, there was come on the bed sheets. And, you know, the stickiness made me feel that the dream was very positive.

GOEBBELS: Excuse me, I've just seen Wolfgang Liebeneiner over there. I need to discuss with him our latest film project, which coincidentally is about euthanasia.

FRITZ: Liebeneiner! I thought his "BISMARK" movie was superb. Awe-inspiring. So, he is making a film about our work? Can we know what it is to be called?

KARL: And do I get a starring role?

GOEBBELS: I can not say too much at the moment. We are still trying to decide on the most sensitive and effective narrative approach for preparing the public's acceptance of euthanasia. But I can tell you the film will be called "I ACCUSE". And I will be asking hospitals to assist with providing patients to work as extras. We will do screen-tests to find the most pathetic, grotesque and

imbecilic looking. The visual argument must
be very persuasive.

KARL: Oh, so I don't get a starring role?

GOEBBELS: Please excuse me.

*(GOEBBELS walks away, pauses for an aside to the
audience)*

GOEBBELS: What's the difference between the injection
and the doctor who administers it? None,
they are both pricks!

Scene 4

*(HEIDE, HELMUT and SIEGFRIED are making baskets.
They could be the Three Norns weaving Man's fate.)*

HELMUT: Heide, why can't people fly?

HEIDE: They can, in aeroplanes.

HELMUT: They can't like birds can. And they can't
swim under the sea like fishes can.

SIEGFRIED: Yes they can, in U-Boats.

HELMUT: Ah but without them, they'd be sunk.

SIEGFRIED: True.

HELMUT: How fast can people run?

HEIDE: Depends. Probably 10 - 15 miles an hour.

HELMUT: Who the fastest animal?

HEIDE: The Cheetah, at 70 mph.

HELMUT: That's because he cheats. *(laughs at his little
joke)* If a man runs from a lion, can the lion
catch him?

HEIDE: Oh easily.

HELMUT:	And from a pack of wolves?
HEIDE:	He hasn't a dog's chance.
HELMUT:	He has with a gun.
SIEGFRIED:	But that's cheating.
HELMUT:	A man cannot fly, he cannot swim, he cannot run, he has no claws, he has no fangs and he cannot climb like a monkey! What is he?

HEIDE and
SIEGFRIED: **Useless!**

HEIDE:	He is the most physically im-perfect of all God's creatures.
SIEGFRIED:	The most disabled.
HELMUT:	Then why is Man the Boss of the World?
HEIDE:	Ah now, that's the thing. If he had been perfect he might have become extinct long ago. Because imperfection makes you struggle, gives you problems, which makes you think, forces your imagination to work, demands creativity from you. Because all the other creatures could get food and defend themselves more easily than Man, they were content, and got lazy and so stayed as God made them. But Man couldn't fly but wanted to, he couldn't swim underwater and wishes he could. So ambition and ingenuity created by physical imperfection enabled him to use his disability to become Lord of the Earth.
SIEGFRIED:	If the Bad Man succeeds in creating Perfect People, then all of Man will cease to exist.

(KARL enters with GOEBBELS, accompanied by LIEBENEINER / Fritz. KARL is showing the pair around the hospital. LIEBENEINER is fascinated by the physical

*appearances of our STORY TRIO, who are made to
parade and pose before him. HELMUT enjoys himself as
he willingly pulls grotesque faces for the movie camera.
SIEGFRIED and HEIDE are not so co-operative.
GOEBBELS stands apart, watching, feeling
uncomfortable. He can't stand being with other disabled
people. He's hoping he won't be noticed. But HELMUT
spots him, smiles and waves. GOEBBELS tries to ignore
him. HELMUT will have none of it and walks right up to
him, and puts his arm around GOEBBELS' shoulder,
who is cringing with embarrassment. HELMUT looks him
up and down, and then stares at GOEBBELS' club foot)*

HELMUT: What happened to you?

*(GOEBBELS says nothing, trying not to see HELMUT's
smiling face)*

HELMUT: What happened to you?

*(GOEBBELS tries to move away, but HELMUT follows
him)*

HELMUT: Why have you got a funny walk? What
               happened?

GOEBBELS: Please, could someone attend to this
               defective. He's getting over excited. Please.
               He might mess himself.

HELMUT: Your foot, you Dummy. He's a Dummy. He
               doesn't know what's wrong with him.

*(KARL comes to GOEBBELS rescue and returns
HELMUT to SIEGFRIED and HEIDE who both grinning.
As KARL escorts GOEBBELS and LIEBENEINER off
stage, LIEBENEINER turns and winks at Our Trio)*

LIEBENEINER: Out of the mouths of babes, eh?

Scene 5

(KARL and FRITZ enter)

FRITZ: How did the gassing tests go?

KARL: Superbly. I took the final results to the Fuhrer yesterday.

FRITZ: Dr. Hermann Pfannmuller still twitters on about starvation. I was visiting his institution last week and we were discussing this issue and he picked up this starving nearly dead 3 year old child and dangled it by the legs, and declared, laughing his head off - "This is the most simple method".

KARL: Hermann is a brilliant psychiatrist who has become brutalised. There is no need for that sort of behaviour. But listen... we had this gas chamber built for us by the SS criminal police.

FRITZ: The SS especially built it for you? That is amazing!

KARL: I exaggerate. It was already constructed and they just lent it to us for the experiment demonstration. But they are going to help us build our first ones at Hadamar, on the same model. The chamber is arranged to resemble a shower room, complete with benches.

FRITZ: How does it work?

KARL: An SS chemist inserts the gas from the outside into the water pipes and it's released into the so-called shower-room through small holes in the pipes.

FRITZ: Sill carbon monoxide?

KARL: Yes but I'm sure we can come up with
              something better though. We had 20 pieces,
              naked of course, in the chamber at a time and
              once the gas was released they quickly
              toppled over or simply lay on the benches. It
              was very good. All instantly dead without
              scenes or commotion. Afterwards, the room
              was ventilated within 5 minutes and the SS
              men removed the corpses using special
              stretchers which mechanically shoved them
              into the crematory oven. All done without
              any contact. Marvellous.

FRITZ: Who operated the gas?

KARL: The SS doctor, of course. I think it will
              always have to be a doctor operating the gas.
              We had a good crowd, watching the
              demonstration. All of us from the T4
              program. Dr. Irmfield Eberl, our new director
              of the Brandenburg killing centre, was so
              enthusiastic, he asked if he could operate the
              gas and took over subsequent killings in the
              demonstration.

FRITZ: So you're converted to gas?

KARL: Well, you cannot argue with the results.
              Anyway, the Fuhrer settled the matter for me.
              I was still uncertain when I went to him
              yesterday. I described both methods to him.
              He then asked which was the more humane
              way? I replied "Carbon monoxide gas, of
              course." - "Then let us use carbon monoxide
              gas as the killing method" he responded in
              his most benign fatherly manner.

Scene 6

BRUNHILDE: It was awful. When I went to buy supplies, everywhere I went in Limburg, I felt people pointing at me, whispering, crossing themselves like I was an angel of death. Of course, ever since my injuries I have been stared at and I will never get used to it - but here in Limburg it was different. Then this old woman came up to me and asked if I was going to Hadamar. I didn't know what she was talking about. She said Hadamar was a small town about 10 miles away. She said that I should run away, escape while I had a chance. Otherwise I would be caught and sent to the baking ovens in Hadamar. And then she was gone. I asked some school children if they knew anything about Hadamar and asked me if I had seen the special buses with the black windows, which go to Hadamar three or four times a week. I nearly told them I'd been in one but my instinct warned me not to, so I simply said I had seen the vehicles. They then replied that whenever they see one of the buses they chant "There goes the murder box again!" - "What do you mean?" I said. - "To take the crazy people to be killed in the pressure steamer!" And then they too ran away. Suddenly my soul felt very alone and very frightened and I wanted to cry. I realised Hadamar was where we had been turned away from. But once the paper-work was sorted I knew we would return. I understood then why Fritz tried to stop me from accompanying my patients. He knew more than he was letting on. And now I had a dilemma. Do I tell my friends what I've been

told? What's in store for them. But what
difference will it make if they know. It won't
change anything. We can't do anything.
Besides, perhaps they already know, or
suspect. Why else do they insist on telling
each other such morbid stories. Oh god, I
don't want to live anymore.

HELMUT: It's your turn Brunhilde!

BRUNHILDE: Is it? Already?

HEIDE: We thought you looked so miserable.

SIEGFRIED: We'd make it your turn again. You can keep
the story positive.

HELMUT: Yes. Tell us about the Hero. He's one of us
now.

BRUNHILDE: Yes...well...

(silence)

BRUNHILDE: ....The Hero... he...

HELMUT: Yes? He? Did he stay long in hospital?

BRUNHILDE: Um...yes...At first...it was hard for him to get
better. He just didn't want to live any more.
He was so depressed about losing his arm
and his eye...

HELMUT: And two fingers!

BRUNHILDE: Yes...he just wanted to die.... he thought he
would never be able to see again... perhaps
he hoped he would never be able to see
again... perhaps he didn't want to see what an
evil wicked world this was... perhaps at last
he knew, he finally knew... and that life was
a waste of time. And that God was the Devil.

(The others look at each other, confused, surprised)

SIEGFRIED: Brunhilde, are you alright?

BRUNHILDE: Pardon? Yes. I'm fine. I.... sorry.

HELMUT: Did he have many visitors?

BRUNHILDE: Pardon?

HELMUT: The Hero! Did he have many visitors in hospital?

BRUNHILDE: Yes. Lots and lots. He had always been popular. Generals came to see him. Bishops. His loving wife came everyday. Then one day, a very famous and clever and good surgeon who knew the truth, came to warn him. Told him that if he didn't get better soon the Bad Man would take him away and cook him in the baking ovens at Hadamar... *(she laughs slightly dementedly)*

SIEGFRIED: What?

HEIDE: Where's Hadamar?

BRUNHILDE: Oh... Hadamar? Nowhere really. Just a name I made up. Anyway, when the Hero with his one good eye read the secret files the surgeon gave him, which proved that the Bad Man was murdering anyone who -

SIEGFRIED: You didn't make Hadamar up. Didn't you say we were in Linburg?

BRUNHILDE: Yes.

SIEGFRIED: Well, Hadamar is a small town from here.

BRUNHILDE: Oh really. What a coincidence!

SIEGFRIED: Brunhilde, can I have a word with you.

(SIEGFRIED and BRUNHILDE go to one side)

SIEGFRIED: Coincidence rubbish! You know something, Brunhilde. What is it?

BRUNHILDE: I don't really. It's just rumours. Bits of gossip I was picking up. But even the children are talking about it.

SIEGFRIED: What?

BRUNHILDE: That in Hadamar is a centre where people are secretly taken to be killed.

SIEGFRIED: What sort of people?

BRUNHILDE: Our sort of people.

Scene 7

(CLAUS von STAUFFENBERG is in his hospital bed. He is wearing a patch over his right eye. His right arm has been amputated. At his bedside are two visitors; PROF. FERDINAND SAUERBRUCH of Berlin University (i.e. FRITZ), and GENERAL HENNING von TRESCKOW of the Home Army (i.e. KARL).)

(CLAUS has just been reading files the conspirators have brought him)

CLAUS: If what you tell me and what I have read here is only a fifth true, and I cannot doubt it since these documents have come from impeccable sources -

TRESCKOW: The Secret Service with the support of its boss, Admiral Canaris, and his deputy Dohnanyi who is one of our principle conspirators, have been compiling these reports for years -

CLAUS: Then our Fuhrer is more monstrous than even I ever imagined. Slaughterhouses for all those judged worthless. The sick, the infirm, the blind...

SAUERBRUCH: The deaf, the deformed, the feeble-minded, the mentally ill. And many of these people you and I would regard as lucid and responsible. The statistics are horrendous. In one killing centre alone, Hartheim, 30,000 victims. At Hadamar in one year they murdered 10,000. In fact they actually celebrated the ten thousandth as a mile stone.

TRESCKOW: Read the report from one of the employees who joined in the festivities!

CLAUS: *(reads)* "Doctor Berner, he had come especially from the Chancellery, gave us employees each a bottle of beer and adjourned to the basement. There on a stretcher lay a naked male corpse with a huge hydrocephalic head. He was put on a sort of trough by the cremation personnel and shoved into the oven. Markle the administrator made himself look like a sort of priest and gave a mock burial sermon. There was lots of music at the celebration which degenerated further into a drunken procession through the institution grounds."

SAUERBRUCH: By the end of 1941 nearly a 100,000 beds had been "emptied". A third through medications, i.e. drugs and injections, and the rest through gassings.

CLAUS: But where will it end Professor Sauerbruch? Who will be the next target?

SAUERBRUCH: Indeed. Our old folk are trembling - and saying "Please don't send me to a state hospital, I don't want to be killed because think I'm a useless eater."

CLAUS: And what about soldiers who contract incurable diseases or are simply wounded while fighting for the Fatherland?

TRESCKOW: Soldiers are already asking this question, and here is the proof that they have every reason to be alarmed - In January 1942, 30 T4 doctors, nurses, office personnel taken from Hadamar and Sonnenstein, under the leadership of Herr Brack went on a "Top Secret" mission across the Russian border to Minsk to perform euthanasia on our soldiers, our boys, severely wounded or brain damaged.

SAUERBRUCH: Admiral Canaris also believes that this Hadamar medical team was also sent to set up the first death camps in Poland. Since then, with the experience learned, expertise and technology developed from the Euthanasia Program, it is estimated that at just one extermination camp nearly 13,000 Jews are gassed and cremated in one day. If you add all the camps together, and that this production line killing has been in operation for nearly 9 months - well the numbers of Jews wiped out, obliterated, just don't bear thinking about. My medical profession - the profession I have devoted my entire working life to - a noble and humane profession - has given this fiend the inspiration, the personnel, the tools to...to ...to - (*he stops, overcome with emotion*)

(CLAUS lays his hand on SAUERBRUCH's shoulder)

SAUERBRUCH: I'm sorry... I.. and the worse thing is that in the beginning I too was a most ardent Nazi supporter. But now I just want this man destroyed.

CLAUS: Surely, there must be other doctors who feel
                as you do?

SAUERBRUCH: Yes but never enough. Gottfried Ewald has
                refused to participate. The Bonhoeffers who
                have given much of the euthanasia
                information to the Abwehr. And Professor
                Hans Gerhard Creutzfeldt of Kiel, a staunch
                anti-Nazi, has managed to protect most of his
                patients. Dr. Kuhn has also refused to
                participate. And I understand that some
                nurses and ward-workers have frequently
                warned patients to leave hospital or have
                helped them to hide. I also know that
                Professor Paul Gerhard Braune wrote a
                personal letter to the Fuhrer demanding that
                the Reich cease immediately this conscious
                systematic elimination of the helpless. And
                the reply he received was a 10-week spell in
                a Gestapo jail.

CLAUS: I would say he got off rather lightly!

SAUERBRUCH: He has powerful friends. Besides, he
                promised not to undertake further actions
                against the Reich.

TRESCKOW: Then, of course, there's the Church, both
                Catholic and Protestant clergy leaders have
                been extremely critical. They were having to
                deal with a lot of unease and unrest from
                flock members who have been told that their
                loved ones have suddenly and inexplicably
                died in hospital.

SAUERBRUCH: Yes, the Bishop of Munster, Clemens Count
                von Galen, he delivered a powerful attack on
                the Nazi's euthanasia policy from his pulpit.

(GOEBBELS and MAGDA / Eva enter, doing a tango dance. Throughout the following dialogue they energetically dance back and forth across the stage)

GOEBBELS: Martin Bormann thinks the Bishop's deserves the death penalty but is afraid that under the current circumstances of the war, the Fuhrer is unlikely to order this measure - since he cannot afford to antagonise the Church.

MAGDA: What can be done to combat this infernal priest?

GOEBBELS: I fear that if something were done to the Bishop, we may as well write off the population of Munster for the duration, and probably all of Westphalia.

MAGDA: When the war is over, will the Fuhrer smash the churches once and for all?

GOEBBELS: Yes, he has so assured me. Christianity, he said, has no place in the New World Order. It is an effeminate and whingeing religion fit for Jews and Moaning Minnies. We will create a new religion, manly and noble for a new German people.

MAGDA: I hear Himmler has recommended that this T4 Euthanasia program be ended, since this secret operation is no longer a secret.

GOEBBELS: Jesus, it has been incompetently handled. Would you believe ashes in urns have been sent to inmates' families who were not their relatives. Or two urns have been sent instead of one.

MAGDA: I heard a story of a family who were told that their loved one who had already had her appendix removed, has subsequently died of appendicitis! Makes you shudder. Will our little Heide be safe when she goes into hospital next week?

GOEBBELS: Don't worry, my sweet. I am arranging for her to go to the best private sanatorium in the country.

SAUERBRUCH: People were bound to become suspicious when families all over Germany were simultaneously receiving letters announcing deaths of patients who were known to be physically healthy on arriving at a particular institution. So, the Fuhrer fearing growing adverse public reaction actually ordered the termination of the Euthanasia program three weeks after Galen's protest.

CLAUS: So the mercy killing has ceased?

SAUERBRUCH: As an officially sanctioned program, yes. But as we have shown you, widespread killing continues to this day but just much more quietly. Doctors are being encouraged to act on their own initiative, their own personal and ideological inclinations, in deciding who of their patients should live or die. The gassing operations have stopped. They were too obvious. Doctors have returned to using drugs, injections and starvation.

CLAUS: But the gassings have stopped?

TRESCKOW: No, the Jews are still being gassed. But that is a racial issue and our German public will lose little sleep over that. Most will, probably, silently, abhor it but it doesn't affect them personally in the same way enforced euthanasia does. The German

people are hardly likely to rise up against
Hitler because Jews are being killed.

CLAUS: Which is why we must do what we have been
              wanting to do for so long.

TRESCKOW: For the Jews?

CLAUS: Not just for the Jews. But for the helpless and
              weak. For the doctors and the soldiers. For
              all of us Germans. For humanity. I have
              decided. I agree with you, General Tresckow.
              All these years I have sought a legal solution.
              I have resisted your constant urgings. But
              you were right and I am bitter, very bitter
              that my squeamish reluctance may have cost
              thousands, possibly millions, their lives.
              Hitler must die. And it will be at this hand,
              this maimed hand that I have left. I swear on
              everything I hold dear, I will personally kill
              Hitler.

(SAUERBRUCH gets up to leave)

SAUERBRUCH: I'd better leave you two to it.

(He exits)

TRESCKOW: Claus, you can't be the assassin. We need
              you to mastermind the plot and execute the
              plan for taking military control once Hitler is
              dead. The Gestapo have neutralized or
              arrested most of the brains and driving force
              of the resistance. Last year we made three
              attempts, and each time we either failed to
              get close to him or the bomb didn't go off.
              And with each failure the Gestapo's net gets
              tighter. We need a leader the Gestapo would
              never suspect.

CLAUS: Because I am now a cripple?

TRESCKOW:	Yes, to be brutally frank. But you must get out of hospital soon. I'm arranging for you to be appointed General Olbricht's Chief of Staff. In no time, you'll be running the Home Army single-handedly.
CLAUS:	*(smiles)* Ho ho very droll.

Scene 8

(SIEGFRIED and BRUNHILDE are having a game of CHESS.   SIEGFRIED is looking at her concentration)

SIEGFRIED:	Brunhilde?

(She moves her knight)

BRUNHILDE:	Check!
SIEGFRIED:	*(startled)* What? Oh!

(He thinks for a while and then makes a countermove)

SIEGFRIED:	Brunhilde. I've been thinking. And I....
BRUNHILDE:	What?
SIEGFRIED:	What you said. What you suspect. Of course, we've sort of known all along. Heide has been keeping up the research. Me, I'm not a reading person. I get bored quickly. I'm an ideas man. I have hundreds of ideas. None of them ever really amount to anything. But all my fantastic day dreams keeps my brain ticking over. Heide and I could see it coming but because we are so alone and powerless we turned it into a game of make-believe. If I could escape I would but I can't. I am a cripple, I cannot walk. Period. My bones are like glass. A child could over-power me. No. I don't want your pity. I'm just stating the

114

hard facts. I am dwarf-like and my body is so deformed that I could not disguise myself. I cannot escape.

BRUNHILDE: I'll help you. If you're not too proud. I could make you look like a toddler.

SIEGFRIED: No. It wouldn't work. All it would do is put you at risk. You can and must leave. I have to accept that I am doomed to die - either in the next few days, or in the few weeks. I... suppose death can't be all that bad - since we all have to do it eventually. The great and the small. Even the Bad Man - Hitler - there, I've said his cursed name. Even Hitler must die, eventually. So that is something for someone to look forward to.... - But What Really gets me - What I really hate - is that some Fucking bastard thinks I am such a worthless piece of shit, that I do not deserve to live - that I am unworthy of life. Not because of what I've done, not because I've robbed, raped, murdered. I have done none of those things. How could I? - The community protected itself against me the day I was born. I am condemned to die because I was born so different that people fear and loath me. And they don't even know me. They condemn me because of the way I look, which offends their dreams. As I said, I'm not saying all this because I want you to feel sorry for me or to help me escape. But... I do want you, need you, to help me... I need you... get my revenge on Hitler and those like him who want to stamp out our kind, those engineers of the Master Race...

(BRUNHILDE moves closer to SIEGFRIED, touches his hand)

SIEGFRIED: I know I have no right... I wish I could have been more expressive but emotions, feelings have a vocabulary I could never master. Never needed to - or wanted to. Daren't. A life time of institutionalisation is hardly an appropriate training ground for expressing affection or love. Doctors, nurses, they are trained to be detached, not to empathize or give warmth. Anyway, they come and go. No sooner do you get attached to someone than they move on. And your fellow inmates, your friends - well, intimate relationships are strictly prohibited and if you try - again someone is moved. So in the end you harden yourself, cut yourself off emotionally, you fear to take emotional risks.

(SIEGFRIED nervously puts his other hand on BRUNHILDE's arm)

SIEGFRIED: When.. I saw you - a part of me - a secret stubborn part that still yearned to be a normal feeling human being - went into rebellion and demanded to be acknowledged.

BRUNHILDE: *(softly)* What part was that?

SIEGFRIED: The part that fell in love with you. I knew I couldn't really hope for your... but...and so I covered it up with the usual immature responses...

BRUNHILDE: Shhh. You don't need to say any more.

(SIEGFRIED looks at her, not daring to believe the love he thinks he sees shining in BRUNHILDE's eyes. She bends forward and kisses softly on the lips. The resulting passion was like a dam bursting)

SIEGFRIED: Brunhilde, do you really love me?

BRUNHILDE: Yes, my precious.

SIEGFRIED:	Truly?
BRUNHILDE:	Yes.
SIEGFRIED:	And you know... what I... I want to come out of our...love?
BRUNHILDE:	Of course, my baby. It's not come as a complete surprise to me. I've been toying with the same idea the last few days.
SIEGFRIED:	The same! You're joking! Serious?

(BRUNHILDE nods and holds SIEGFRIED close to her)

SIEGFRIED:	Even though you must know what it means?
BRUNHILDE:	They are wrong to think what they think. You can't have perfection in a world that is **living.** The only perfect thing is silence. And stillness. So, the only thing that's perfect is nothing. The world if it is not to stagnate, seize up, dry up - become a dust bowl, needs people like you, Heide, Helmut. People say there are only seven colours in the rainbow. Well, when I look at the rainbow I can never see where one colour exactly ends and another exactly begins. It seems the colours blur into another in an infinity of gradations. I will not let Hitler deprive the world of your inheritance. So, with what little power we have, lets conspire - and possibly perspire - to thwart his petty-minded plans. I'll have your baby and all its so-called decadent genes, and if he or she is born disabled, then I won't have lost you.

Scene 9

(HEIDE and HELMUT are sitting together, with picture books)

HEIDE:	Are you ready?
HELMUT:	Yes.
HEIDE:	Are you sure you can remember?
HELMUT:	Yes.
HEIDE:	It is very important that we remind ourselves of our own secret special history.
HELMUT:	Yes.
HEIDE:	You mustn't be upset if you get it wrong or can't remember.
HELMUT:	No.
HEIDE:	Who was a great Roman Emperor, and was one of us?
HELMUT:	Julius....
HEIDE:	Julius who?
HELMUT:	Julius Caesar.
HEIDE:	Why was he one of us?
HELMUT:	He had fits.
HEIDE:	He was an epileptic. Who was another Roman Emperor who was one of us, who conquered England?
HELMUT:	Claudius. He was like you. A spastic.
HEIDE:	Yes, we're sure he had cerebral palsy. Who was a dwarf, and so one of us, who helped destroy the Roman Empire when it got too big for it's Jack-boots?
HELMUT:	Um... Was he a German?
HEIDE:	Sort of.
HELMUT:	I know. Attila the Hun.

HEIDE:	Yes. And who was a Viking and conquered half of England, but couldn't walk and had to be carried into battle on the back of a shield.
HELMUT:	Ivan the Bonkers!
HEIDE:	(*giggles*) No. Try again.
HELMUT:	(*giggles*) IVARR the BONELESS. He was like Siegfried wasn't he?
HEIDE:	Yes, he also had brittle bones.
HELMUT:	What if his men dropped him?
HEIDE:	They didn't dare. They needed his brains, to win battles.
HELMUT:	He's in love.
HEIDE:	Who, Ivarr the Boneless?
HELMUT:	No. Siegfried. And Brunhilde. They love each other.
HEIDE:	(*visibly disturbed*) How do you know?
HELMUT:	I know. Are you sad?
HEIDE:	Don't be silly. Come on, who was paralysed down all one side of his body, couldn't walk properly and yet was the greatest Tartar conqueror since Genghiz Khan?
HELMUT:	Er. Timmy the Lame.
HEIDE:	Yes, Timur the Lame, or as the English called him Tamburlaine.
HELMUT:	Why was his name changed?
HEIDE:	Because his enemies don't like to be reminded they were thrashed by a cripple. And who was one of the most important leaders of the French Revolution who had a clubbed foot?

HELMUT:	No more.
HEIDE:	Just two after this. Please.
HELMUT:	The Liar? Jokey Gobbler?
HEIDE:	No, not the Liar.
HELMUT:	Can't remember.
HEIDE:	Talleyrand.
HELMUT:	Oh yes. No more.
HEIDE:	Two more. Please. Who was a great German revolutionary who could have stopped the Bad Man, but was cruelly murdered by her old comrades?
HELMUT:	What do you mean?
HEIDE:	She couldn't walk properly, and people who use to like her, had her killed? Over 20 years ago?
HELMUT:	Rosa. Red Rosa!
HEIDE:	Yes. Rosa Luxembourg. One more now. Who is one of us, has a wheelchair and is the President of America and might fight the Bad Man?
HELMUT:	Is he real?
HEIDE:	Who?
HELMUT:	The Bad Man?
HEIDE:	Yes. I'm afraid so.
HELMUT:	I don't want to play any more. (*suddenly very frightened*) Where's Siegfried and Brunhilde?

Scene 10

NINA: Claus was impatient to get started. He tells
         General Olbricht, head of Army General
         Office, that he expects to be fit again within
         3 months. By early May, he has learnt to
         write with his left hand. I tried to persuade
         him to slow down. He was still very weak.
         But, as usual, he wouldn't listen. Doktor
         Lebsche and I tried to get him to agree to
         have an artificial arm made and fitted but he
         refused. He said this would add too many
         weeks of hospitalization and he couldn't
         spare the time. And by late September he was
         out and began his official duties at the
         O.K.H. in Berlin. He was to supply trained
         replacements to our armies at the field, which
         he performed with such extreme competence
         that he was rapidly promoted to Chief of the
         General Staff. It is ironic that Claus who was
         secretly organising a coup d'etat, should so
         impress Hitler that he should remark - "At
         last, a Staff Officer with brains!"

TRESCKOW: As you know, "Operation Valkyrie" was
           designed by Admiral Canaris as a cover
           operation to crush a rebellion by foreign
           workers in any of our cities - particularly,
           here in Berlin. But, of course, in reality, it is
           designed to capture power the moment Hitler
           has been assassinated. Within the first two
           hours of his death, we must seize control of
           the means of communication. If this is not
           possible, we must at least render inoperative
           the major signals centre. Particularly at
           Hitler's H.Q. That has to be knocked out.

CLAUS: We're going to need troops to capture the
         Berlin broadcasting station.

TRESCKOW:	Yes, and we need troops to guard our centre of operations here at the Bendlerstrasse from counter-attack by the SS and possibly by units of Goering's anti-aircraft troops. We will have to rapidly render harmless the large numbers of SS troops in and around the capital.
CLAUS:	Well, at least the chief of the Berlin police, Count Helldorf is with us, so we can rely on them to deal with the SS.
TRESCKOW:	We've also got available the elite tank units of the Guard Battalion, the Artillery School and the Armourer's School, as well as two battalions of home guard infantry.
CLAUS:	Within 50 miles radius, we've got 8 other possible sources of combat troops which could intervene on our behalf very speedily once they realise the tyrant is dead.
TRESCKOW:	Hmmm. Yes, well, we will have to give marching orders to some of these units an hour or so before Hitler is assassinated to ensure they arrive in Berlin at the vital moment.
CLAUS:	Obviously, at the start, they will be told that they are on a training exercise.
TRESCKOW:	Of course. But when they arrive, Hitler will be dead and they will be available to seize control and arrest the other leading Nazis.
CLAUS:	Goebbels, especially. That evil slug is usually in Berlin.
TRESCKOW:	And then there's the Home Army, your domain. How many people have we got there?

CLAUS: Quarter Master General Wagner has been with us all along. Also artillery General Lindemann. He can be relied upon, once the balloon has gone up. There are at least ten others who are committed anti-Nazis. Those who aren't and refuse to co-operate we arrest. I do have replacements lined up just in case. For example, if my boss, Col. Gen. Fromm doesn't play ball, then Col. Gen. Hoepner has agreed to step in.

TRESCKOW: Excellent. We will need to have similar arrangements throughout the Reich and abroad, with particular attention to Paris and Brussels.

CLAUS: I'm still concerned that we haven't come up with a decent plan for actually killing Hitler. Which, not to put a too fine a point on it, is the be-all and end-all of the whole bloody operation. Our biggest problem is his inaccessibility. I know you refuse to consider this but the fact is I'm one of the few conspirators who has occasional access to him. None of your suicide bombers have got near him. We tried to send some one armed with a gun but he was stopped, told "No adjutant officers today." and turned away.

TRESCKOW: Sure, damned bad luck. But Claus, when the rebellion breaks out you will be needed here in Berlin, to keep a tight rein on the coup. Remember, I'm not going to be here.

CLAUS: Even so, it has to be me. I am never searched. Everyone else is but I'm not. Why? Because I'm disabled. Lets use it. Their preconceptions are preventing them from considering me a potential threat. I am the perfect assassin. We haven't got time for any more botched attempts. Every failure brings the Gestapo closer. There are arrests everyday. They know there is a conspiracy a foot. I can feel the noose tightening. Secondly, it has to be now. We are losing the war on both fronts. The Russians will reach Berlin before Christmas, I'm convinced of it. If we kill Hitler and stop the war now, we stand a better chance of securing a more favourable peace with the Western Alliance. It is essential that we Germans act before Germany is reduced to mere geographical rubble.

TRESCKOW: Claus, you can no longer handle a gun, and it could take too long to train your left hand.

CLAUS: Forget the gun. A bomb in my brief case...

TRESCKOW: That's suicide.

CLAUS: Not necessarily. Listen. I'm not arguing anymore. Last week, when I was at Hitler's H.Q., do you know what I heard him say - If he, Hitler, falls, then the whole German nation should not survive him. He plans to destroy us all - out of pure nihilistic spite. He says that if we Germans cannot win his war, we do not deserve to continue to exist....

(Karl as TROTT arrives)

TROTT: I think I've got some good news. The Western Alliance will deal with a new German government, but they insist on a simultaneous surrender in the East.

TRESCKOW: No problem. That can be organised.

TROTT: But they still won't modify their "unconditional surrender" slogan.

CLAUS: Alright. Tell them we accept. All that matters
           now is that it is we Germans who deliver
           Germany from its shame. In four days time, I
           have another meeting with Hitler. And in
           four days time he will be dead.

Scene 11

(The Story Circle reconvene)

HEIDE: For the next four days, Our Hero feverishly
           worked....

HELMUT: Like a demon possessed!

*(GEORGE is on the far left of the stage simultaneously
making a bomb, using the "Anarchist Cookbook" as his
guide. On the far right is JONAH / CLAUS who is also
making a bomb. Sometimes the actor is JONAH talking to
GEORGE, sometimes he is CLAUS assembling his bomb)*

HEIDE: ...preparing his bomb and fitting it into his
           brief-case, using dynamite confiscated by the
           German Secret Service from British
           saboteurs sent over to bomb our munitions
           factories.

HEIDE: Our Hero's bomb had a 10 minute fuse. This
           was a small glass capsule, and every day he
           practised with his one hand operating a tiny
           pair of pliers, resembling sugar tongs. These
           were needed to break the capsule in the fuse
           which would start the time bomb.

(CLAUS practises with pliers)

BRUNHILDE: So he's only got 10 minutes to get away?

HEIDE: Yes. He has a car waiting, with its engine
           running, to take him to an aeroplane he's
           stolen.

HELMUT: Yeah!

(With the Bomb set, GEORGE becomes SIEGFRIED and rejoins the Story Circle)

HEIDE: At last the day arrives. The day we've all been waiting for. Our Hero is summoned by the Bad Man to give his report, and so Our Hero travels with the bomb to the Bad Man's Lair....

HELMUT: Yeah, the Dragon's Lair!

HEIDE: ....which is heavily guarded by soldiers and a circle of mine fields. The Hero gets to the first check point, but he isn't searched. He gets to the second checkpoint. And he isn't searched. He gets to the third checkpoint and gets out of his car. And the guards still don't search him. He then enters the Bad Man's Bunker and someone offers to carry his briefcase but he says no, very politely and then goes into the toilet...

HELMUT: Why, does he want to wee?

HEIDE: No. He wants to start the time bomb which is still in his briefcase. Wrapped in a shirt. He takes the bomb out and breaks the capsule. Now he's got just ten minutes. He goes into the Bad Man's conference room where the Bad Man and all his Bully Boys in Black are discussing the War. With the Bomb ticking away, Our Hero puts it under the table, near where the Bad Man is standing. Our Hero quickly gives his report...

HELMUT: I hope it's short..

HEIDE: Yes, its very short and he speaks very quickly... and ... then...It's Brunhilde's turn!

BRUNHILDE: Oh no! Not me. I can't!

126

SIEGFRIED:	Yes you must. The Hero was your idea.
BRUNHILDE:	No seriously. I can't.
HELMUT:	Yes Brunhilde you must. Please. Finish the story for us. Does the Bad Man die and Our Hero escape?
SIEGFRIED:	You're the only one who can make it a happy ending.
BRUNHILDE:	Heide was telling it so beautifully. Besides I..... I know! Why don't we have a vote on it? Does the Bomb go off and kill the Bad Man or does something else happen which prevents the Bomb from killing the Bad Man?
SIEGFRIED:	Alright. Fair enough. Lets have a vote. I say the Bomb fails to go off.
HELMUT:	Ohh! Well, I say the Bomb blows up the Bad Man, and Our Hero saves the Good People.
BRUNHILDE:	I agree with Helmut. The Hero gets away from the Bunker two minutes before it is totally destroyed by the Bomb, killing the Bad Man and his cronies.
SIEGFRIED:	Two to one, so far. Heide, it's back to you. You can either confirm the Yes vote or leave it an open verdict.
HEIDE:	Oh dear. Well, I have never believed in neat happy endings.
HELMUT:	Oh no!
HEIDE:	The real world is no fairy tale. I'm with Siegfried, the Bomb fails to kill the Bad Man. But we're split even. So the story must continue.

(Enter DR. EVA DRECK)

SIEGFRIED: No. I want it to end now. We have to resolve
                it one way or another. We need a casting
                vote. Lets ask Doctor Dreck.

HELMUT: We can't include her in our story. She might
                tell on us.

SIEGFRIED: It's okay, we'll just say we're playing a game
                of lucky numbers. She has to choose a
                number. If it's Even, the Bomb kills the Bad
                Man, and no one tries to destroy us any more.
                If Doctor Dreck chooses an odd number then
                the Hero's briefcase with the Bomb in it is
                accidentally kicked over and moved by
                someone to a different spot under the table,
                where it does explode, killing some of the
                Bully Boys - but not the Bad Man. He is
                merely wounded and shaken. He is, of
                course, very angry. The Hero and all his
                friends are captured, tortured and shot.
                Anyone with the same name as his is killed.
                That is the penalty for failure. Everything
                fails and Germany is doomed to destruction.

BRUNHILDE: God, Siegfried, does it have to be so bleak
                and bloody, so apocalyptic? I didn't know
                you were so Wagnerian!

HEIDE: Ragnarok! The Doom of the Gods!

SIEGFRIED: Yes. If there are no more Heroes and if the
                Gods cannot or refuse to help save us, then
                the Gods deserve to be destroyed. Shall we
                call Dr. Dreck over and have her play our
                game?

(They all say "Yes")

SIEGFRIED: Doktor Dreck! We are playing an imaginary
                game of roulette. Can you help us and be the
                Wheel of Fortune?

HEIDE:	Our Spinner of Fate!
EVA:	My, my. How clever you all are. You must be mind-readers. I was coming over to collect you. I want you all to pack your bags.
BRUNHILDE:	What?
HELMUT:	Where are we going?
SIEGFRIED:	First, Dr. Dreck, will you play our game? All you have to do is choose a number from one to a hundred. Any number. Please.
EVA:	Very well. A number? One to a hundred?
SIEGFRIED:	Yes
EVA:	Very well. Fifty-Three. Now pack your bags.
SIEGFRIED:	Shit!
HELMUT:	Fifty-Three? Is that odd or even?
HEIDE:	Odd. The brief-case is kicked over.
SIEGFRIED:	The Bomb is moved and the Bad Man is saved from the blast.

(BRUNHILDE runs over to DOKTOR DRECK, who is collecting the patients' things)

BRUNHILDE:	Doktor Dreck! Where are the patients going?
HELMUT:	The Bad Man is saved?
SIEGFRIED:	The Hero Dies.
EVA:	*(shouts across to the patients)* Come on. Pack. Move. MOVE!
HEIDE:	Ragnarok. Armageddon.
BRUNHILDE:	Doktor Dreck, why?

EVA:	This sanatorium is getting over-crowded. Our patients have to be moved. Not very far. Just ten miles down the road.
BRUNHILDE:	Ten miles? Oh no. No. NO.
SIEGFRIED:	Hadamar!
EVA:	Brunhilde. Control yourself. Remember, you are staff and you have a responsibility to these patients. You must stay calm. For their sake. I don't know what you have heard, but you must forget it. They must not feel anxious. Pull yourself together and help them gather their possessions. We have no time. The bus is waiting.
BRUNHILDE:	I don't want to. It's murder!
EVA:	(*hisses*) Shut up, you silly little bitch! You must. You will be instantly shot if you refuse, and your patients will still die, but they will die unhappy, and without your comfort.

Scene 12

*(While FRITZ, in SS doctor uniform, in black jackboots, armed with side pistol, addresses the audience, HEIDE, HELMUT and SIEGFRIED undress until they are completely naked. Blank, white, expressionless <u>masks</u> are put on their faces. They form a queue. EVA and BRUNHILDE takes each patient in turn and places them on a stool or chair, where KARL is waiting. EVA fills the hypodermic syringe and hands it to KARL. He injects the patient, who once dead, gets up and goes to the back of the queue. The idea is to create the impression of an **automated conveyer belt of death**. The three actors with their characterless masks repeatedly die 4 or 5 times during the Nazi Doctors' monologues)*

FRITZ:	It was done in a room that was kept locked at other times. The windows were painted white. To the right of the door was a small table - on it, a set of injection needles and syringes; next to these a bottle resembling a thermos flask, containing a yellowish liquid - the concentrated pink solution of Phenol. An inexpensive substance, easy to use and very effective. Also in the room were two stools and on the wall was a hook on which hung a rubber apron. The patient, sometimes two, was brought in and positioned on a footstool so that the right arm covered the patient's eyes and the left arm was raised sideways in a horizontal position. Sometimes the right hand was at the back of the neck, with the left behind the shoulder blade, and a blindfold towel wrapped around the eyes. I hated seeing the patients' eyes as death took them.
KARL:	(*whilst administering the injections*)Sometimes I would stuff the patient's right hand into his mouth to stifle his cries. Like so. (*he forces HELMUT's hand into his mouth*)
FRITZ:	Placing the patients in these positions would thrust the chest out so that the cardiac area was maximally accessible for the injection and to prevent them from seeing what was happening.
EVA:	Initially the phenol was injected into the vein. This gave the whole procedure a nice, comforting medical aura.
KARL:	But we had to change the technique to injecting directly into the heart ventricle because of the greater killing efficiency of a

direct cardiac introduction. When administered intravenously the patient may take minutes even hours to die, whereas thrusting the needle straight into the heart with just 10 to 15 millilitres of phenol solution, he would die instantly or within 15 seconds. Very rarely would death take more than two minutes. Thus it is possible to kill 50 people in less than 2 hours.

FRITZ: This Euthanasia policy gave us, doctors, ample opportunity for research and experiments. Plenty of material to work with. Corpses were immediately transported to anatomy departments at various universities. Preservation of bodies and parts was paramount. Jars were made ready for organs, segments of liver, spleen and pancreas. Whole skeletons, particularly of the most grossly deformed bodies were donated to medical science museums.

KARL: You can not imagine the extraordinary progress in our studies of Huntingdon's Chorea and cancer. Being given total access to these otherwise worthless human specimens was a God-send. Our research results suddenly mushroomed and we German scientists were soon ahead in nearly every field. We all had our own pet projects. I, for example, have a theory that deformities traumatically acquired can be inherited. So if I saw a patient whose cranial shape seemed particularly unusual, I would have him photographed and then I would give him a lethal injection and have him on my dissection table in no time. Needless to say, my ideas are not very popular with orthodox Nazi medical views on pure hereditary.

Now, Doktor Josef Mengele has two passions
- Twins and dwarfs. Mengele! What a
fantastic role model! A very precise, sharp,
brilliant research scientist. You should see
his dissection room at Auschwitz. He has a
dissection table of polished marble, a basin
with nickel taps, porcelain sinks.
Immaculate. I tell you he is even more
obsessed about the genetics of the abnormal
than I am. If he gets his hands on an unusual
hunchback or hermaphrodite, or an entire
family of dwarfs, as he did once, he is
positively beside himself with joy, and is not
seen at large for weeks on end as he studies
them intensely. Ah Auschwitz! I wouldn't
say no to his job. I'd have plenty of rabbits to
toy with there.

*(At this point, HEIDE has arrived for the last time, as a
faceless victim. She takes off her neutral, nameless mask.
She is forced onto the stool)*

HEIDE: I'm human too.

*(She struggles a little. FRITZ is summoned to help
restrain her)*

HEIDE: **I'm human too**!

*(EVA nervously pours the liquid onto a dish. KARL is
getting impatient)*

HEIDE: *(screams)* **I'm human too!**

*(HEIDE struggles more violently. FRITZ is having to get
more forceful. EVA, with shaking hands, fills the syringe.
KARL snatches it from her and rams it into HEIDE's
chest, who jerks and whispers...)*

HEIDE: I'm human, too.

*(HEIDE slumps forward - **dead**. EVA is severely rattled. BRUNHILDE is crying. KARL refills the syringe, and sends FRITZ to fetch HELMUT)*

(HELMUT is brought in, sees the syringe and screams, ripping the mask from his face)

HELMUT: No! I don't want an injection. I don't like injection! I've been a good boy.

(His struggling and screaming becomes more wild. FRITZ has great problems with controlling HELMUT, who is physically stronger than HEIDE, and so resorts to violence, hitting him. BRUNHILDE picks up a stool to attack FRITZ, but is seen by EVA, who stops her, as FRITZ pulls out his gun and pistol whips HELMUT about the face. KARL yells at FRITZ)

KARL: Sir! You will stop that now! I will not have damaged goods!

HELMUT: No injection. Please. No!

(EVA grabs BRUNHILDE and shakes her)

EVA: Brunhilde. Please. Help Helmut. Make it easy for him. Calm him. Do your duty. Help him to pass peacefully.

(BRUNHILDE, sobbing, slowly nods and goes over to the weeping and frightened HELMUT. She takes him in her arms, and rocks him gently, singing quietly "Lilly Marlene")

BRUNHILDE: "Time would come for roll call,
Time for us to part....

HELMUT: Stay with me, Brunhilde. You won't leave me?

BRUNHILDE: No, Helmut, my sweet. I will be with you forever.

"Darling I caress you and press you to my heart...

(KARL signals to EVA to administer the injection. She goes on her knees and pushes the syringe into HELMUT's chest)

BRUNHILDE: "And in the power of lantern's light,
I hold you tight as on our last night...

HELMUT: Why are you crying? Don't cry. I'm your...

*(HELMUT slumps into her arms - **dead**)*

BRUNHILDE: "My... my Lili...

(BRUNHILDE breaks down, weeping inconsolably and rushes of stage)

(SIEGFRIED is next in line. EVA pulls away his mask and is about to inject him when KARL stops her)

KARL: No, not this one. He's to go to Auschwitz. Dr. Mengele wants him. The good doktor is obsessed with dwarfs.

EVA: But Siegfried isn't a dwarf?

KARL: Mengele knows but he wants him all the same. Wants to do a comparative study. Try out a few experiments. See what differences there are in responses. He needs him alive for a while.

(Meanwhile SIEGFRIED notices that the unused syringe is lying unattended. He snatches it and plunges it into the unsuspecting back of KARL, straight into the spinal column)

SIEGFRIED: **DIE! HELL-HOUND, DIE!**

(KARL swings round, horrified, desperately trying to remove the syringe, but realises he's doomed, and drops dead. FRITZ pulls out his gun, places it at the back of

SIEGFRIED's neck and pulls the trigger. SIEGFRIED is instantly killed. BRUNHILDE on hearing the yells and gunshot, rushes in, sees SIEGFRIED dead and screams hysterically. FRITZ swings round to shoot her but EVA blocks him and grabs BRUNHILDE, pushing, urging her away)

EVA: (*whispers*) Go on, get out of here! Run. Escape while you can. They won't miss you. Go underground.

(BRUNHILDE leaves and EVA returns with an empty syringe)

FRITZ: Where's the screaming bitch?

EVA: In the other room. I gave her an injection.

FRITZ: Silenced her for good, did you?

EVA: Yes.

FRITZ: Thank god for that.

Scene 13

(EXPLOSION)

(GOEBBELS on the telephone in his Ministry office)

GOEBBELS: But this is appalling, my Fuhrer. ... How can this be?....Who would have the audacity to do such a thing? - Claus von Stauffenberg? ...That one-eyed colonel! ... But are you unharmed? ... Some minor scratches. Thank providence for that. Yes. Certainly I will. Right away. Yes. A radio announcement. There has been an attempt on your life, but mercifully it has failed...Yes. I will have this broadcast as soon as possible. ..Yes, now. Do

we know if others are involved? ..
Sorry...Yes...Of course, Fuhrer, you still have
Mr. Potato-Head with you. Ha ha . Yes, yes,
it's a very good name for Mussolini.
Certainly. Very well. And again, thank god
the terrorist swine failed.

(GOEBBELS hangs up. He is stunned and almost close to tears. Pulls himself together and looks out of the window and is startled by what he sees)

GOEBBELS: Good god! We are being surrounded! The
swine have organised a little putsch! Right,
well, we'll soon see about that!

(GOEBBELS reaches for the telephone and speaks into the receiver)

GOEBBELS: It seems we have an uprising on our hands.
There has been an attempt on the Fuhrer. No.
He is perfectly safe. Send word to Major
Remer. I want him here at once. If he is not
here within 20 minutes I will assume he is a
traitor or being held by force. Either way, in
20 minutes I will order the SS troops to
attack and capture his headquarters.

(Puts the phone down, then picks it up again)

GOEBBELS: I want SS troops to cordon off the
broadcasting station. It must be secured
within ten minutes. Also I want the rebel
stronghold to be located. The rats must be
hiding somewhere in this city. I don't care if
Schellenberg is out carousing. Find him and
order him to locate the rebels and smash
them. JUST DO IT! *(slams phone down)*

(The phone immediately rings)

GOEBBELS: What? What! Panzer divisions moving in on
the Tiergarten! Jesus. The filth are more

organised than we realised. But they must be
fools. To act when the Fuhrer is not dead.
Send someone to talk to the Tanks'
commander. He must be told the Fuhrer is
not dead, and order him to turn his guns on
the traitors.

*(GOEBBELS slams phone. He returns to his desk and
starts to write the Radio Announcement. The phone
interrupts him and snatches up the receiver)*

GOEBBELS: What now? ..Has he indeed! Come to arrest
              me! Good. Send him up.

*(Enter Fritz as MAJOR REMER, flanked by two of his
troops, played by KARL and EVA)*

GOEBBELS: Ah Major Remer. So good of you to call.
              Another few minutes and I'd have the SS
              bombard your headquarters.

REMER: Doktor Goebbels, I have come to arrest you.

GOEBBELS: *(smiles)* Really? On whose authority?

REMER: Since Hitler is dead, and the SS discredited,
              we have a new provisional government under
              Colonel Stauffenberg...

GOEBBELS: Ah yes. Stauffenberg! Where is
              Stauffenberg? Why is he not here arresting
              me? Has it not occurred to you that he is
              lying? Because, you see, the Fuhrer is NOT
              dead.

REMER: You lie.

GOEBBELS: You fool, you have been misled. I insist,
              Hitler is very much alive. So rejoice!

REMER: *(now uncertain)* You're a liar. You're a
              natural born liar. You're the most notorious
              liar of our age!

GOEBBELS: (*smiles sweetly*) Thank you. I'll take that as a compliment.... Major Remer, I see you are wearing the Knight's Cross, First Class.

REMER: Yes.

GOEBBELS: A very high decoration. Not given lightly. Only the brave receive those. Did the Fuhrer give you this honour?

REMER: Yes. The Fuhrer personally bestowed it upon me 3 weeks ago.

GOEBBELS: Did he? Congratulations! So, if you were to hear your Fuhrer's voice, you would recognise it?

REMER: Yes...but... (*points gun uncertainly at GOEBBELS as he picks up the phone*)

GOEBBELS: Give me a Lightning connection to Hitler.... Ah, my Fuhrer... I have a Major Remer here who seems to think you are dead and has come to arrest me... Yes, of course.. (*hands the phone to REMER*) ..Your Fuhrer would like a word with you.

REMER: (*uncertain*) ...Yes my Fuhrer... yes my Fuhrer. I do. Your voice is unforgettable... Yes my Fuhrer. I will crush the rebellion. Stauffenberg is as good as dead. I'm 27 sir. Thank you sir. Thank. That is a great honour! (*hands phone back to GOEBBELS*)

GOEBBELS: Promotion?

REMER: Yes. I'm now Colonel Remer. The Fuhrer has said that I'm to take orders only from Himmler, General Reinecke and you...

GOEBBELS: Right. First, lift your troops' blockade of all government buildings. Second, halt all troop movements into the city. Inform their officers they have been deceived. Third, provide me with an armed escort. I have to get to the broadcasting station. And finally, bring me the head of that one armed, one eyed bungling colonel. And Colonel Remer... Congratulations!

Scene 14

NINA: Neither the SS, Himmler, Colonel Remer nor Goebbels managed to capture my husband alive. When his boss, Colonel Fromm, realised that Hitler was still alive, he knew the coup had failed and he had Claus and three of his comrades arrested, gave them a summary court martial and had them taken to a court yard outside the O.K.H. building and shot by a firing squad....

(CLAUS is lined up in front of a pair of spotlights - i.e. car headlights)

CLAUS: I beg the world accept our martyr's fate as penance for the German people.

*(Rifle shots ring out and CLAUS collapses - **dead**)*

NINA: ...Five minutes later, the SS arrived. They were furious to find my husband had already been executed. Colonel Fromm was later shot. The aftermath of my husband's failure to kill Hitler was terrible. It was a bloodbath. Over 7000 people were arrested and put on trial. 5000 were eventually executed. Nearly a 1000 were killed simply because they shared the name Stauffenberg. Men, women, children. In no way related to Claus. Hung on meat-hooks. Their torture and death filmed as a warning to others. Hitler had taken his vindictive, murderous insanity to depths that

not even Hell could reach. And me?
Amazingly, I survived, with my children.

Scene 15

(HITLER / Karl, who is in a bit of a mess, i.e. right ear heavily bandaged, right arm in a sling and right trouser leg ripped off, is helped limping onto the stage by GOEBBELS. HITLER stands facing the audience, collecting himself. GOEBBELS hands HITLER his radio speech)

HITLER (KARL): A very small clique of ambitious officers, devoid of conscience and at the same time criminally stupid had forged a conspiracy to remove me... I was spared a fate which held no horror for me, but would have had terrible consequences for the German people. I see in it a sign from Providence that I must and therefore shall, continue my work.

*(As HITLER speaks, out of the shadows emerge HELMUT, HEIDE, SIEGFRIED and BRUNHILDE. They hum and buzz like droning aeroplanes. SIEGFRIED stops and becomes GEORGE and goes off to the far left of the stage, to finish making his bomb. Meanwhile, still buzzing, HELMUT takes a long ribbon from CLAUS who has slowly risen, and with arms outstretched like plane wings whirls around HITLER and GOEBBELS. HEIDE taking a long ribbon, does the same. So does BRUNHILDE and CLAUS. All whirling and zooming around, like annoying flies, irritating HITLER and GOEBBELS alike, who are becoming more and more entangled in the ribbons as they are being wrapped and drawn closer together. They try to resist but it is useless. They are sucked into each other's vortices, until they are finally bound tight against one another. HEIDE hands them each a cyanide pill, which they swallow and sink to the floor, **dead**)*

(BRUNHILDE steps forward and faces the audience)

BRUNHILDE: Nine months after Claus von Stauffenberg's failure to kill Hitler, nine months after his execution, nine months after the deaths of Helmut, Heide and Siegfried, the Bad Man and his Liar killed themselves. They couldn't face the truth that their evil ideas made them the most useless eaters of them all. Three days after Goebbels' suicide and four days after Hitler's, I, having succeeded in escaping to England, gave birth to Siegfried's child. A gorgeous baby girl. I named her Lucia, the Queen of Light. I call her Lucy. In mid-winter, we Teuton and Nordic people have a bonfire festival of Santa Lucia, where we invoke the return of the Sun, and call upon the Bringer of Light to herald a new dawn. A new Spring, to sweep away the long darkness. And thus it is I so named my little Lucia. And yes, I'm proud to say - she **is** disabled. Just like Siegfried.

(BRUNHILDE turns to GEORGE who has just finished making his bomb and about to set the timer)

BRUNHILDE: George. Please. Don't take up the bomb and the gun. I know you fear it is all starting up again. Yes. Your Thatcher did sneak in a eugenics law, the Fertilisation and Embryology Bill in 1990, which, yes, does permit the murder of disabled nine-month old foetus'. And yes, I know your doctors and many parents are demanding the right to murder so-called severely disabled children. And where will it end?

(BRUNHILDE walks over to GEORGE and kneels at his side, putting an arm on the bomb, and looks into his face)

BRUNHILDE: George. I know you want to kill the MPs that
               voted for the eugenics Bill of 1990. You
               want to kill the genetic scientists, you want to
               kill those doctors who have recently
               murdered severely disabled babies, and you
               want to kill the parents that asked them to do
               so. You want to teach them a lesson before it
               is too late. But such extreme measures are no
               longer necessary. We now know how to
               make the world realise, without all this
               childish violence, that they exterminate
               people like you and Brigit and Steven
               Hawking at humanity's peril..

*(GEORGE staring back at BRUNHILDE, slowly shakes
his head)*

BRUNHILDE: Listen to your old grandmother. Because I
               know. I have lived through it all....

*(BRUNHILDE gets up and slowly walks up stage away
from SIEGFRIED, looking at him. The SPOT LIGHT on
her, fades to black, as she backs away to disappear into
the past)*

*(GEORGE raises his hand, poised to set the clock ticking
- He looks up at the audience , looks intently at them -will
he or won't he? ...... Sudden Blackout)*

THE END

of this Play

APPENDIX

(This paper was originally written for the Department for Education and Employment's enquiry into barriers preventing disabled people's professional participation in the performing arts)

DISABILITY AND THE PERFORMING ARTS
- There is No Fair Play -
by Nabil Shaban, a disabled performer

The Prologue:

David Rappaport, a talented comic actor who also happened to be a dwarf, committed suicide in 1990 by shooting himself. The scene of his death was beneath the Hollywood sign. Clearly, this was an act of protest and disillusionment. I accuse Hollywood and the entertainment industry in general of his untimely demise. Typical of the treatment performers like David Rappaport who are discriminated against because of physical aesthetics is exemplified in the case of the movie "Time Bandits" where Rappaport and fellow dwarves never get a billing or reference in TV listings. Their major role is ignored or regarded as a vehicle for making the "normal" stars look good. Just before he died, David told me that Terry Gilliam, the film's director, during the shoot, would shout "Bring on the dwarves" with a smirk and a sneer. It humiliated David. It would be like Attenborough when shooting "Cry Freedom" saying bring on the niggers when requesting the black actors...or Ridley Scott during "Thelma and Louise" yell out "Bring on the bitches" or John Ford shout "Bring on the jews" if requiring the jewish actors. David mistakenly believed he could become a Hollywood superstar as a dwarf....he should have realised that show business is too Body Fascist to allow that to happen. David or me could have all the talent and charisma in the world but we will never become matinee idols because the world has been brainwashed into believing our bodies are not the stuff of romantic movies.

145

There are barriers for disabled people who want to start or continue (after they have become disabled) working in the performing arts.

"Body Fascism", a term I created in 1983, which places a value on a person's worth on the basis of physical appearance or attributes....thus someone with an able body that appears perfect, fit, handsome or beautiful, has a superior status...whereas a person who deviates from a socially or culturally physically acceptable norm...i.e. too fat, too thin, too short, physically deformity e.g. hunchback, wasted hand, clubbed foot, impaired in mobility or senses (blind, deaf etc)..."ugly" in some shape or form....are deemed to have an inferior status. Consequently, the heroic, the romantic, the good, the desirable are portrayed/represented by performers whose physical or bodily attributes evoke the greatest sympathy / identity from the largest possible audience. Producers of the performing arts, if they want....or are forced (through lack of government subsidy or incentives or sanctions etc).... to maximize profits either through box office sales or audience ratings, believe they cannot afford to alienate the greatest potential audience with content that places the disabled performer in the central or key role. Basically, the performing arts is organised, structured, motivated by the market imperative of giving the arts and entertainment consuming public what they want. If the dominant consumers of the performing arts are young, white, male, able-bodied who want stories about the beautiful and the handsome and the physically perfect, then it is, and has been, much more difficult for disabled people to work in the performing arts. Equally, this is also a problem for women, elder citizens and ethnic and racial minorities. The problems of Sexism, Ageism and Racism in the performing arts are particular aspects of Body Fascism. "Body Fascist" Market Forces are not just a problem for disabled people.

One of the barriers for disabled people starting out in the performing arts is due to access to training.

Drama schools etc, will only audition/interview and give places to aspiring performers who physically fit a pre-conceived mold of the "perfect" performer in terms of physical appearance and physical abilities. Drama schools claim that they can only accept as students those who they consider to stand an excellent chance of obtaining employment after graduation....thus applicants who are perceived as too fat or ugly or physically inept or disabled and therefore of little marketable value, will not be accepted for performing arts courses. Where the majority of performing arts training institutions are concerned, criteria of talent and motivation come second place to desirable physical attributes.

Another problem for today's drama schools is that the training syllabuses have a heavy emphasis on able-bodied movement and physical agility...the courses are designed with the assumption that all students can stand, walk and run on two normal legs, that they have normal hearing, sight and speech. The movement, dance and fight training do not take into account physical differences. Drama schools argue that it is pointless accepting disabled people for performing arts training, as they would not be able to effectively participate in many of the mandatory courses.

Some of the barriers are of a practical nature - for example, restrictions on physical access to buildings or communication difficulties.

For people with mobility difficulties, steps and stairs are obvious barriers. Restrictive width of door frames, heavy fire doors, height of door handles, inaccessible entry-phones, electronic pass-points. Restrictions on access to studios, performance spaces. Lack of accessible dressing rooms, make-up, costume departments. Inaccessible toilets and shower facilities backstage. Similarly, technical equipment may be inaccessible for people who have restricted or no hand/finger dexterity, e.g. cameras, recording devices, editing facilities with small buttons and controls. Even where there are lifts, the push-buttons might be beyond the reach of a wheelchair user. Also for people with sensory impairments, barriers to the performing arts are posed by communication difficulties, e.g. information on notices that are not conveyed to the visually impaired, or lack of induction loop systems for the hard of hearing.

However, barriers of a practical nature are never sufficient to prevent active participation in the performing arts, where there is the will on the part of the producer to employ the disabled performer. For example, recently I worked as an actor at the Royal national Theatre....and because the venue and director were determined to include me in the cast, appropriate adaptations including accessible toilet/shower and dressing room were created for my personal benefit. Equally, I have on three previous occasions, worked at the old Royal Court, which was not wheelchair-friendly backstage, but because the demand for my performing services was great, every effort was made to remove the barriers to my employment. Similarly, when I have worked in film and television, sometimes in difficult studios and foreign locations, the production strenuously endeavours to minimise barriers to my involvement. For example, film companies, invariably provide me with an Access Worker.

Where there's a will or financial incentive, there's always a way....and excuses surrounding problems of a practical nature seem to always mysteriously disappear. When a producer is negatively prejudiced towards employing a disabled performer, then problems of a practical nature become convenient opt-out clauses.

Fire regulations or problems of insurance cover were/are another convenient excuse for not employing disabled performers.

Ultimately, barriers of a practical nature are the product of ingrained attitudinal barriers.

Other barriers are due to difficulties with attitudes towards role portrayal - for example, seeing the disability rather than the person's talent.

The performing arts and entertainment industry is primarily concerned with telling stories....and within the story-telling conventions, it is not considered socially or culturally acceptable or appropriate for the principal protagonists to be "ugly" or disabled. If a disabled character is central to the story, then the performer playing the role must appeal to the widest possible audience, with the invariable casting consequence of the role being played by a non-disabled actor. Producers seem to believe that the dominant non-disabled audience need disability to be sanitized, rendered less threatening or disturbing through the medium of non-disabled performers or stars. Hence, we have Daniel Day Lewis playing cerebral-palsied Christy Brown in "My Left Foot" or Al Pacino playing the blind key character in "Scent of A Woman" or Helena Bonham Carter in "Fear of Flight". In an industry where the star-system, the product of market forces and "Body Fascism", prevents disabled performers from playing leading disabled roles, its not surprising that it is even harder for disabled performers play roles where disability is not the issue. In those rare situations where disabled performers play central roles, the producers always ensure that the narrative has a non-disabled lead character who reflects the interests and sympathy of the majority non-disabled audience. This also allows the producer cast a non-disabled star. Generally, these productions tell the story of the "problems" the disabled protagonist causes the non-disabled protagonist....so, we see the disabled person through the trials and tribulations, and consequently, through the learning experience of the non-disabled parent or non-disabled spouse. Thus, for example, Bernard Hill's character in BBC's "Skallagrig" or the abused wife of paraplegic in Lars Van Treer's "Breaking the Waves" (a film I consider to be highly offensive to disabled men).

Disabled performers suffer from the entertainment industry's attitudinal prejudices on at least two counts. First, roles rarely portray disabled people as lovers, mothers, fathers, romantic, heroic (other than the boringly predictable "overcoming" illness or disability). A disabled person could be a private detective, a barrister, a forensic psychologist (I have a degree in psychology) a spy, a smuggler, a contract-killer, a pilot, a taxi-driver, a UFO or ghost investigator....yet, such opportunities are never forthcoming.

Secondly, popular (i.e. commercial) entertainment which overly concentrates on police or hospital dramas, or period costume dramas inevitably denies employment opportunities for disabled performers. Where the central characters are police detectives or doctors and nurses what roles are there remaining for disabled performers? Villains? Victims of crime? Sick patients? Hardly positive role models for disabled people. And what opportunities for disabled performers in yet another Shakespeare or Dickens or Bronte? Even in Richard III, the one major disabled Shakespearian character, one is unlikely to find a disabled performer playing the role. whereas black actors, have played the Moor, Othello... and Jewish actors have played Shylock. In the discrimination stakes, disabled people are the lowest of the low....

Disabled people live and work in the community, and yet you wouldn't think so, if you thought television soaps were an accurate depiction of life in Britain today. I live on a council estate, go to the local pub and shop at my Asian grocery store just around the corner. I have a local girlfriend, who is not physically disabled but culturally inhibited in that she is a Pakistani Muslim, and so not free to have an open relationship with a disabled white non-Muslim man. Yet where is this existence of mine depicted in Eastenders or Coronation Street or Brookside etc?

The BBC were once very daring and adventurous by casting a disabled performer in a leading role in one of their soaps "Eldorado"....Julie Fernandez, an actor who has the same disability as me, and uses a wheelchair, looked set to pave the way for other soaps...until the "hate mail" from Sun-type readers / neo-Nazi viewers, who complained that she shouldn't be allowed to live, let alone be allowed on television. Such a response seemed to have frightened the BBC off the idea of having disabled people featured on mainstream, prime-time television. The BBC and Channel Four, forced by the Government and market forces to be ratings conscious, are providing less and less opportunities for disabled performers.

As British television and film industry is pressurised to pander more and more to the lowest common denominator (in an attempt to be more popularist and therefore commercial) so disabled performers will be increasingly excluded from job opportunities and media representation, with the effect that anti-disabled attitudes will continue in society.

Role portrayal by disabled people is not just an issue within drama. Instead of the Government spending money on an advertising campaign telling people to see the person not the disability, the money should have been spent as incentives and sanctions, pressurizing advertising agents to employ disabled people in television commercials selling such things as Coca-Cola, Rover cars or Levi jeans or Chanel perfume. If I don't see disabled people advertising these products, why the hell should I buy them....they are obviously not meant for people like me.

These problems are more widespread in some areas of the performing arts than in others.

In my experience as a disabled performer, I have found that the bigger the budget or expense of a production, the less likely a disabled person will be included in the cast....or the more commercial the enterprise the smaller the role for the disabled performer.

I have played the leading roles in theatre which is subsidized or require less funding and therefore not dependent on maximum box office receipts.....whereas my roles got smaller in television which needs to be more commercial....and even smaller, often cameo roles in film where the investment is greatest. The more money put into the venture, the less risks the producer is prepared to take.

I have played Hamlet and other romantic leads, Jesus, Khomeini, Haillie Selassie etc on stage (particularly in the alternative, fringe arena) where the profit imperative is not paramount, consequently, directors are more adventurous, creative, daring....because there is less to lose if the production isn't commercial.

In television, I have more rarely played leading roles (my romantic lead in Channel Four's "Deptford Graffitti was a notable exception) but had in the past, played substantial supporting roles....that was until television during the late Eighties became too ratings-conscious. I have always thought it significant that the most commercial television channel, ITV, has never given me acting work. In fact, Granada back in 1988 would not allow an independent producer, they had commissioned, to cast me in the leading role of a children's drama series "Microman" because the television executives believed my physical disabilities and being in a wheelchair would frighten the child audience. It was said had the project been a single drama they might have allowed such creative casting but to risk the investment of a seven part series on a disabled performer was not worth taking.

I have noticed that the BBC and Channel Four, since they have become more populist, employ me and other disabled performers less and less. Now, I am lucky if I am offered cameo roles and one-liners.

Likewise, with big budget commercial movies, I am offered smaller roles, usually the disabled stereotypical roles of cowardly dwarf or pathetic begging cripple. Often I am offered "signpost" acting roles...i.e. my character's sole function is to point the main protagonist in the right direction.

I am considered a talented enough actor to play Hamlet on stage but not on television or in the movies.

In the early Nineties, the production department of the British Film Institute started to seriously consider making movies about disability issues with disabled actors in leading roles, or films by disabled writers and disabled directors. I was commissioned by the BFI to write a feature film about disabled people being exterminated in Nazi Germany. Before I could write the second draft, BFI production was disbanded and then absorbed into the new monolithic Film Council....whose brief is to only fund commercially viable films. Suddenly, just when I thought things were looking up for disabled people in the British film industry, the rug was unceremoniously pulled from under our wheels and white sticks, yet we are being shoved out in the cold again, by populist, market imperatives.

In short, in those areas where the performing arts are most heavily subsidized, tend to lie the greatest opportunities for the disabled performer.

In addition, there is the fact that performers with certain types of disabilities find it more difficult to find employment, for example:
People with severe facial disfigurement.....or with severe speech impairment.... or body deformities. Wheelchair users if they "look" disabled. People who need walking aids.

Disabled performers who are "attractive-looking" and can look as if they might be "able-bodied" in a wheelchair.....or can look as they are "normal"....have greater employment opportunities.... e.g. deaf people, blind people, people who normal mobility but have a deformed hand or arms, people with a slight walking impairment (the actor, Jasper Britten is a case in point....although of course, he has the added advantage of having a famous actor father). Basically, those disabilities that have less difficulty finding employment are ones where negative Body Fascist criteria least apply.

Also, some disabilities require less expenditure to facilitate access, so producers looking to keep costs or practical inconveniences down, will, if they MUST employ a disabled performer, opt for the cheapest disability.....

***To deal with the barriers for disabled performers in finding
suitable employment, I suggest the following:***

A combination of carrot and stick is probably the most
effective way of removing barriers for disabled performers in
finding suitable employment. Over the past twenty years,
subsidies, grants, funding from regional arts boards and Arts
Councils, and stipulations from the Lottery has done more to
enable disabled people to become professionally involved in
the performing arts. If the Arts Council of England didn't fund
the Graeae Theatre Company of Disabled Performers, most of
today's disabled actors would never have got their first break.
Equally, if the Scottish Arts Council and the Lottery Fund
weren't committed to promoting disabled people's employment
in the theatre, Edinburgh's Theatre Workshop wouldn't be able
to create Britain's first fully integrated professional theatre,
offering two years contracts to five disabled actors and five
non-disabled actors.

Subsidies, grants, tax breaks, funding incentives from the
State, from arts bodies and trusts, the Film Council,
commercial sponsorship are all carrots to encourage the
employment of disabled performers. But what about the stick?
The Anti-discrimination legislation should allow disabled
people to sue or prosecute producers if non-acceptance for
performing role is the result of Body Fascist prejudice. Also,
producers and directors should be penalised for casting a non-
disabled person in the role of a disabled character, since
disabled performers are being deprived of employment. There
should be a Discrimination Surcharge, which could be
collected to fund projects giving employment to disabled
performers. For example, since 10 percent of the population is
said to be disabled, then one ought to see a 10 percent presence
of disabled people in theatre, film and television productions.
Equally, 10 percent of television commercials should include
disabled performers. ITV companies, the BBC, Channel Four,
organisations like the Institute of Practioners in Advertising,
should have their annual output assessed for equal disabled

representation....if disabled performers are found to be less than 10 percent present, then the offending organisations should be financially penalised. Repetitive offenders should not have their franchise renewed.

Equally, as with Lottery funding, grants for project or revenue funding should only be given on the condition that a minimum of 10 percent of the cast is made up disabled performers. Thus, companies like the RSC, and the Royal National Theatre should not receive state subsidy if they do not significantly include disabled performers in their productions. (In fact, I think to truly reflect today's western society and culture, 10 percent of all leading roles should be played by performers with disabilities, just as 50 percent of all leads should be played by female actors). Why should I as a disabled person pay taxes to help fund so-called national theatre (after all, I am part of the nation) which has no bearing on my own life, when I don't see people like me on the stage, telling stories that I can identify with. Similarly, why should I pay a television license fee, when the bulk of the BBC content has so little relevance to me. I don't want to see endless dramas, soaps, comedies where good-looking, white, able-bodied males always having relationships. It just makes me feel inferior, and hate being disabled, which is something I cannot change. Performing arts today, television commercials etc bend over backwards to redress the balance with respect to gender representation. Generally, it is not good practise to depict women in such a way that women viewers are made to feel inferior or inadequate. In fact, one often finds, particularly in a TV commercial, the female character proving to be smarter than the male counterpart....this is known as positive compensatory stereotyping....and it is currently all the rage in gender role reversal politics. To a lesser extent, we see the same treatment within the racial context. Black performers are far more in evidence and play more positive roles than say 15 years ago. Sadly, the same cannot be said for disabled performers, not as a representative ratio. It is hard to believe that it is nearly 20 years since the International Year of Disabled People (IYDP 1981), and yet there seems to be so little progress with respect to a just and fair representation of disabled people in the performing arts. The main reason for this retardation is the two pronged Thatcherite attack of cut backs in social services, and draconian reduction of arts funding; and the "dumbing-down" and over-emphasis of commercial viability of the media output.

The Epilogue.

Historically, religion, charity, the medical profession and literature and the arts are all responsible for promoting negative attitudes towards disabled people.....

Religion suggests that disabled people are not whole people who need to be healed, are blemished people, described in the Old Testament as an abomination in the sight of God...disability is often portrayed as the result of a sin, bad karma, a punishment from God...disabled people are often despised, or pitied because of certain religious beliefs. Generally, Christianity, Hinduism, Islam, Judaism...do not enable disabled people to feel good about themselves.

Charity perpetuates negative responses to disabled people because in order to appeal for money, the disabled person must appear pitiful, needy, inferior, begging, pathetic....what charity does to persuade people to voluntarily part with money, is massage their egos, allow them to feel superior in relation to the recepient....this is their reward for making a donation....a reward at the expense of the needy disabled person, who is having to degrade themselves so that the benefactor can feel good.

Medical Profession sees the disability and not the person...objectifies the individual as a disease, as a clinical problem, seeks wholeness, exploits the disabled person as a "lab rat", as a meal ticket to international conferences, doctors perceive disabled people in terms of what they cannot do as opposed to what they can do, what the person lacks rather than capabilities, the disabled person is defined in terms of their physiological aberrations. The medical model does not allow the disabled person to feel good about themselves.

Literature and the Arts throughout the ages and across cultures generally present a negative image of disabled people. Hunchbacks, dwarfs, scarred or deformed people, cripples are used in fairy tales, myths and legends, fiction to denote evil or other negative human qualities such as cowardice, impotency, greed, envy, revengefulness. From Richard the Third to Captain Hook, from Long John Silver to Quasimodo, from Rumplestiltskin to the Ugly Sisters....from the cuckolded paraplegic in Lady Chatterly's Lover to James Bond villain Dr. No. From Bosch to Breughul, Hell is peopled with the deformed. In the modern era, the tradition is continued with the movies and theatre, perpetuating the myth of deformity and disability as a metaphor for evil...e.g. Scar in "The Lion King", "The Phantom of the Opera", the scar-faced bad Yank in "Platoon", Freddy Kreuger in "Nightmare on Elm Street" and so on. Our literary and artistic culture does not make it easy for disabled people to be comfortable with their condition.

Even the history books marginalize the persecution and attempted systematic extermination of people with disabilities. Compared to what has been written and portrayed about the Jewish Holocaust, how many books, plays, films and television dramas can be named depicting the Nazi Euthanasia Program....where the gas chambers were originally designed and constructed to destroy "useless eaters", Hitler's term for the sick, crippled, deformed, the genetically degenerate. The Disabled Holocaust has been side-lined because society would still like to see us, disabled people, dead.

And now, the euthanasia debate, the genetic sciences with the eugenic implications add salt to the wounds. Today, more than ever, we disabled are being made to feel we do not deserve to exist...with the Fertilisation and Embryology Bill allowing disabled foetuses to be aborted at full term, implying that if a foetus is deformed or disabled, it is not a human life worthy of life....is not even human....with genetic research, genetic engineering, genetic and embryo screening paving the way for Genetic Cleansing....disabled people are being made to feel more inferior than ever...society is being encouraged to view disabled people as inferior, a blot on the landscape, undesirable, life unworthy of life.

It is not surprising, given all this prejudice stacked against disabled people, that disabled performers have difficulties in gaining employment in the areas of the performing arts. It is not surprising that producers of the performing arts have negative attitudes towards disabled performers....that sponsors and investors and broadcasters can not see the commercial value of disabled performers...because the public for centuries have been conditioned to regard disability in a negative, bleak, depressing and loathsome light...that two legs good....one or no leg, BAD....

Dr. Nabil Shaban   *- May 2000 -*